BLOOD

IN THE

SOIL

BLOOD
IN THE
SOIL

A TRUE TALE OF RACISM, SEX, AND MURDER IN THE SOUTH

CAROLE TOWNSEND

Skyhorse Publishing

Skyhorse Publishing books may be purchased in bulk at special discounts for sales promotion, corporate gifts, fund-raising, or educational purposes. Special editions can also be created to specifications. For details, contact the Special Sales Department, Skyhorse Publishing, 307 West 36th Street, 11th Floor, New York, NY 10018 or info@skyhorsepublishing.com.

Skyhorse® and Skyhorse Publishing® are registered trademarks of Skyhorse Publishing, Inc.®, a Delaware corporation.

Visit our website at www.skyhorsepublishing.com.

10 9 8 7 6 5 4 3 2 1

Library of Congress Cataloging-in-Publication Data is available on file.

Cover design by Rain Saukas
Cover photo credit Thinkstock

Print ISBN: 978-1-63450-751-6
Ebook ISBN: 978-1-63450-752-3

Printed in the United States of America

ACKNOWLEDGEMENTS

MY MOST SINCERE thanks to:

Detective Michael Cowart, who so graciously spent hours with me recounting his meetings and experiences with Joseph Franklin. With skill, finesse and eloquence, he brought the stories to life.

The late Mr. Gene Reeves, attorney and magistrate Judge. His openness and honesty, and his passion for the law, inspired me.

Gwinnett County DA Danny Porter and his staff, who opened their offices and the case files to me, giving me clarity and accuracy in piecing together this true tale. Without Mr. Porter's introduction to Mr. Cowart, I would not have had access to the wealth of knowledge and experience of the lead investigator.

Mr. Paul Cambria, long-time attorney for Mr. Larry Flynt, for spending time with me, helping me understand the nuances of the obscenity trial, for sharing his eyewitness account of the shooting, and for giving me insight into the complex character and brilliant mind of Mr. Flynt.

Captain Jeff Smith, Lawrenceville PD, for taking the time to provide photographs and back stories about Gwinnett County, then and now. What a gentleman.

Dr. Taher Bagheri, for sharing with me the grueling hours of surgery immediately following the shooting that nearly killed Flynt and seriously injured Reeves. Another gracious gentleman.

Judge Dennis Still, Attorney and Chief Municipal Court Judge, Lawrenceville, for his early remembrances and introductions.

Gwinnett Historical Society, for preserving the colorful and fascinating fabric of Gwinnett County.

Mr. John Vaughn, and the Vaughn family, for two things: the use of their beautiful beach home (the perfect place to write), and for their remembrances. They are some of the finest people I am privileged to know and amazingly, they are also distant relatives of the same Vaughns about which I write in this book.

And of course my wonderful husband **Marc**, whose patience and support never fail me.

The most beautiful works of art, in my opinion, are tapestries, for they are woven together from the threads and fabrics of many sources. A tapestry always tells a story. —CT

CONTENTS

AUTHOR'S NOTE

WHILE RESEARCHING THE history and events contained in this book, I had the benefit of many interviews—conversations with some of the actual men and women who were there as the story unfolded. One of those men was Detective Michael Cowart, retired, Gwinnett County Police Department. Mr. Cowart spent hours with me, pulling out and dusting off memories that I know were difficult for him to revisit. Because of his uncanny memory and riveting eloquence, I have told much of this story from his perspective, with his permission. Whether paraphrased, quoted directly, or summarized in my own words based on his accounts, Cowart's stories are just that: his stories, based on his recollections and memories. He brought those stories to life in the manner of a true and gifted storyteller.

In writing about Joseph Franklin, I based my accounts on both written and recorded interviews, including taped interviews between Cowart and Franklin. His mannerisms and quirks I gleaned from articles, old news clips, and recollected accounts from Cowart and other law enforcement officers. The insights into his thoughts and character are based on Franklin's own words, as well as others' observations and opinions of him. Any "filling in" that I have done as the author of this book is based on facts, descriptions, and accounts shared by those who knew Franklin, or on Franklin's own words. Any opinions offered in this book, whether they pertain to the political and social climate of the turbulent 1960s and 1970s in the South, or the character and quality of Larry Flynt's publications, or the opinions and influence of the famous "religious right," are asserted based on the points of view of the characters brought to life within these pages. After all, the crimes and punishments, the shames and victories, that characterized the South during those years were largely fueled by just that—opinions.

In the chapter that sees Joseph Franklin meet his end, I alone have written his thoughts. Of course, no one knew what they were, but I have woven together bits of factual information with the thread of my own imagination and words. I intend no disrespect or dishonesty in doing so. I merely believe that every man's end deserves, at the very least, a look, an observation, and a conclusion. I gave him mine.

A book draws breath and comes to life when the details and nuances of a story are shared just as accurately as the main narrative is written. To that end, I researched the popular music of the time period (late 1970s). I researched the commercials one could expect to hear in between songs on the radio. I researched popular clothing trends, vehicles of the day, and the sights, smells, and sounds of the cities through which we travel in this book.

BLOOD IN THE SOIL is not written about one character in particular; rather, it is the true tale of several characters with very real flaws and strengths, steeped in the rich history (and the flaws and strengths) of the glory and shame of the South. The characters are remarkable, and the volatile South in the throes of change was remarkable. The weaving of the stories within these pages creates a fabric both fascinating and terrifying; it is my sincere belief that it is in the stark and honest retelling of these tales that we can prevent a return of the shame and wickedness that draped like a shroud over the South just fifty years ago.

BLOOD
IN THE
SOIL

PROLOGUE

THE WORDS IN this book stir much of the painful history of the South, history that was often colored with ignorance, hate, and shame. The story of serial killer Joseph Paul Franklin's childhood, young adulthood, and eventual crusade against blacks and other minorities includes some of the worst of the worst of that history.

Degradation, cowardice, and murder did not characterize all Southerners in the 1950s, '60s, and '70s, but they were intricately woven into the fabric of Franklin's life. The story contained in these pages would not be accurate and truthful without giving life to the dreadful, skewed reality that was his.

"I believe that I am acting in accordance with the will of the Almighty Creator: by defending myself against the Jew, I am fighting for the work of the Lord."

—Adolf Hitler, *Mein Kampf*

The devil did, in fact, go down to Georgia.

CHAPTER 1
Jesus Christ Takes Care of Business
(1978)

THE PLAIN-LOOKING MAN in the green Ford Gran Torino popped on his left turn indicator, then checked the driver's side mirror and easily merged into the light Monday afternoon traffic headed south on Interstate 85. He kept pace with the other early afternoon commuters, driving not too fast, not too slow. Checking the rearview mirror, he didn't see anything out of the ordinary behind him. No cars fast approaching, no flashing blue lights. Everything was going according to plan.

Satisfied that he had made a successful escape and the cops were, as usual, a day late and a dollar short, he reached for the radio dial, clicked it on, and listened intently as he slowly turned the knob first right, then left. *Probably won't be anything about it on the news, not yet anyway.* He continued turning the dial through the few stations he could pick up, static crackling through the speakers in between mostly weak signals. He found Gloria Gaynor belting out "I Will Survive," then Grand Funk Railroad urging him to "Do the Locomotion." Further up the dial he passed a fire and brimstone preacher threatening eternal damnation unless listeners sent in a donation pronto, then Paul Harvey telling his listening audience "The Rest of the Story." No breaking news though. That would come soon enough. Satisfied that the events of the day had gone down almost exactly as he had planned, Joseph Paul Franklin decided to pull off the highway for a quick celebration of sorts, a little pat on the back that he believed he had earned. Flipping his signal light on again, he merged into the far right lane, then took the next exit ramp off the highway. At the end of the ramp were several gas stations; he chose the Phillips 66 station closest to the exit. Carefully accelerating, he again indicated a right turn. *Always pays to abide by the law.* The thought made him chuckle to himself. He made another right turn into the station's parking lot and cruised slowly past a few eighteen-wheelers, then past customers at the pumps. He was careful not to look directly at anyone. The pay phones were located at the other end of the lot, and that suited him just fine. He cruised coolly past the other customers and eyed the phone at the far end of Ma Bell's bank of battered and worn telephones. He'd use that one. Pulling into a faintly marked parking spot, he shifted the car into PARK and surveyed his surroundings. He had the area to himself, at least down here by the phone. Not bothering to turn the ignition off, he opened the door, swung his feet out onto the pavement, and dug into his shirt pocket for his smokes. Swiping a book of matches off the dash, he pulled one out and deftly struck it against the back of the matchbook. The hissing flame blossomed; he touched it to the tip of his Marlboro and puffed hard, the blue smoke that escaped curling lazily upward. Enjoying the familiar burn in his lungs a bit longer than he usually did, he exhaled lustily, and a faint smile curled the corners of his mouth. Letting the cigarette hang from his thin, dry lips and squinting his one good eye against the burn, he glanced skyward, following the smoke.

Joe could count on one hand the number of really good days he had enjoyed in his twenty-eight years on this God forsaken earth. Today would go down as one of Joseph Paul Franklin's Top 10 Best Ever Days. Everything had gone off without a hitch, save one small one. In the overall scheme of things, however, it didn't matter one damn bit. *The dude was just unlucky, that's all. Maybe I'll send him a Get Well card.* He laughed aloud at the prospect. *Fucker was just unlucky.* He took another lusty drag on his cigarette as he looked back over his shoulder at the gas pumps and the big trucks just beyond them.

Sitting there in that parking lot, staring up into the brilliant blue sky of an early March afternoon, Joseph Franklin almost looked like a happy man, and if anyone had noticed him, that very thought might have even crossed their mind. But of course, no one did notice him. Not one person.

Time to have a little fun.

Abruptly he stood up, and walking toward the pay phone, he fished a dime out of the front pocket of his jeans. Inside the booth, he picked up the phone book that hung by a chain. Holding the cigarette in his thin lips and squinting to see through the smoke, he opened the book and ran his finger down the listings, looking for one in particular. Finding it, he slipped the dime into the slot, waited for the dial tone, and dialed the number. He gazed out at the traffic speeding by on the interstate. *They have no idea. They will soon enough but right now, they have no idea what just happened.*

"State Court, Gwinnett County. How may I direct your call?" Sara Hutchins was helping her friend Maxim Sims at the switchboard, which had all at once lit up like a Christmas tree with a wave of incoming calls. Maxim was Georgia state court solicitor Gary Davis's assistant.

"Is Gary Davis in?" Later, when she gave her statement to the police officer, Sara would say that the man's voice sounded calm and kind of authoritative, like a preacher's.

"No, I'm sorry, he isn't."

"Well you know that Larry Flynt case? Tell them not to bother sending it to the jury. Jesus Christ already took care of it."

"Wait just a minute, and I'll get his secretary," Sara quickly answered, but before she could finish her sentence, the man with the preacher's voice had hung up; the line was dead.

Joseph Franklin smiled as he gently placed the receiver back into its scuffed Southern Bell cradle. He opened the folding door of the phone booth and walked back to his car, which was still idling richly under the brilliant blue sky. In one smooth movement, he removed the cigarette from his mouth and flicked it onto the pavement, crushing it under his heel. He slipped behind the big steering wheel of the Gran Torino, closed his eyes, and took a deep breath, letting it go slowly as he leaned back into the imitation leather comfort of the seat.

Yes. Jesus Christ had taken care of it, all right.

He backed carefully out of the parking spot and shifted into DRIVE. Time to boogie on down the road.

CHAPTER 2
Opening the Box
(2014)

Detective Michael Cowart

I'm retired now. Doubly retired, in fact, from both the United States Navy and the Gwinnett County Police Department. When I retired from active duty in the Navy, I was second in command of the largest Naval Investigative Service in the world, responsible for the entire northeast quadrant of the US. I was still a relatively young man at the time of my first retirement, so I decided that I wanted to become a cop, to play cops-and-robbers, so I did. I was hired first by the Lawrenceville, Georgia police department and later, by the Gwinnett County PD. As an officer of the law, I served as commander of the Special Investigation Section (narcotics, vice, intelligence, and such). I went on to serve as commander of Internal Affairs, then Precinct, then Division Commander.

All these responsibilities worked to make me, I suppose, distant and apart from many of the men with whom I worked. Too, the formality that had become a part of who I was upon leaving the Navy never left me, but to me, these were not problems. I was always kind of a straight arrow, and I was always very single-minded when it came to the question of why I did what I did for a living. Quite simply, I was a truth seeker.

Finding the truth in any case was all that mattered to me. The duplicity, the politics, the manipulations that reproduce like weeds in our line of work, always disappointed me. I never understood striving for anything but the absolute, honest truth. I am proud of that fact, and I am proud of the men who worked with me, of those who I believe sought the same thing. I suppose that set me apart from most, as well, but there were a few men with whom I worked who were wired the same way. Two of those were Detective Dan Bruno, and Captain Luther Frank McKelvey ("Captain Mac" or just "Mac" to those who knew him personally). In the early 1980s, Mac was Captain of the Detective Division. Eventually he would be promoted to Major, and there was never a finer man or one more deserving of the title. A graduate of the FBI Academy, he had valuable knowledge and skill with respect to profiling. He also had priceless connections to those in the FBI who did such work.

When Joseph Paul Franklin's name first came across the Chief's desk on that first tantalizing letter from his attorney in 1983 (I'll get to that shortly), it only made sense that Mac would be put in charge of the case; he would oversee Det. Bruno's efforts and my own, and as a team we started down the rabbit hole that became just one piece of the massive, national Joseph Paul Franklin investigation. Anyway, that is how I came to know Joe Franklin.

I am retired, which means that all that I have seen and done in service to my country and my community are memories, all of them behind me. My beloved wife and I are comfortable, as are our little pack of wire-haired dachshunds. Our children are grown, and they have given us some wonderful grandchildren. This is my life now, and I do cherish it dearly.

There has never been cause until now to look back, to ponder, to relive any of the terrible things that I have seen first-hand in my law enforcement career. There has been no cause to resuscitate some of the terrible people whose paths I have intentionally crossed in an attempt to bring justice, to reveal truth, to shed light on a world that is darker than most people can fathom—darker than most would want to fathom. I have come to realize, however, in recent weeks and months, that some stories never truly come to an end. Some curtains never close all the way. Some people never really die. Some wrongs are never righted, because at the root of those wrongs is an evil so black and so malevolent that it simply cannot die. The darkness lives on because of its own black energy, its own putrid roots.

This is one such story, one I believed I had locked securely away in the basement, never to go down there again. I revisit it now purely because of a newspaper article that I read, just before Thanksgiving of 2013. It caught my eye, of course, because I knew the man about whom it was written. Some might say that I knew him better than most. The article reported that Joseph Paul Franklin had been executed on November 13, 2013, at the federal prison in Bonne Terre, Missouri. He was put to death by lethal injection. There had been some legal skirmish over that (I would have expected nothing less from Joe Franklin). It had slightly delayed the execution, but the delay hadn't lasted long. He was now as dead as dead can be.

Reading the article opened the door to that dark, dank basement to which I referred earlier, and I find myself now unpacking the contents of that dusty box, locked away long ago, knowing full well that if I were to reach far enough into the box, I could fall in. I could fall into it and come out on the other side. I could find a path, one that had its beginning three decades ago for me, in Gwinnett County, Georgia, and begin to walk it again. I must admit that I hesitated before opening this box, as I did not relish removing the contents and examining them up close, even one last time.

Ah, but reach into that box I did, and eventually I found myself walking back down that path, slowly and tentatively at first, feeling my way through specifics and details that were difficult to recall. But the farther I walked, the easier the details came and soon, they were rushing back in faster than I could sort them out. I do not know what to think about that last; does it mean that I will always be a detective, never truly letting down my guard even in my pleasant retirement with my dear wife and our dogs, children, and grandchildren? Or does it mean that this man about whom I will tell you took a rather sizeable bite out of me, Detective J. Michael Cowart, and the wound has never truly scarred over completely? I suppose that the answer to this and many other questions will best be found if I begin back at the beginning, where my path and Joe Franklin's first crossed.

My work on the case of Joseph Paul Franklin marked a definite turning point in my career and, I suppose, in my life. It was during those years of investigation that I came to understand that not everyone is in the business of seeking and telling the truth. My God, how naïve that must sound, but it is a fact. Until I set out with my colleagues to work the maze of the crimes of Franklin, I never realized the twisted and underhanded motives that drive many people. I learned that even some of the people whom I trusted and respected could be detoured from the straight path, for one of many motives. And I, a grown man who had spent my entire life asking questions and testing the answers, a man who had held heavy responsibility in both of my careers, was heartbroken by that discovery.

I must say, I also fondly and respectfully remember the men who served alongside me, most especially the men with whom I worked diligently to solve this case, to answer the questions, to bury it, once and for all.

In order to understand the mere existence of a man like Joseph Franklin, one must understand the time and place in which he was born and he grew up. Those factors and others, I believe, worked together to create the perfect storm that created him. He was born in Mobile, Alabama, in 1950, and he was born into wretched poverty and cruel abuse. Those truths alone account for much of what Joseph Franklin was made of. Much, but not all.

CHAPTER 3
Preparing for Judgment Day
(1978)

THE MONTH OF March in Georgia is a coy, flirtatious tease, lifting her skirt to show a little glimpse of spring, then coldly dropping it again and storming out in a huff. She can be icy and blustery, or she can scream into town riding on the tails of warm and wet tornadoes, leaving death and destruction in her wake. That was one of the things Joe enjoyed about the South. If you didn't like the weather, you just had to stick around for about fifteen minutes, and it'd change.

The March of 1978 though, was mostly warm and sweet, like a young girl who hasn't yet been jaded by hardship and disappointment. On one day in particular that year, March 6, the sun shone brightly, and cheerful birds chattered back and forth among the pink and white blossoms on the cherry and pear trees, as if gossiping about some delicious secret to which only they were privy. And on the town square in Lawrenceville, Georgia, the first flowers of the spring season—pink tulips and yellow daffodils—swayed in an uncharacteristically gentle March breeze, waving to passersby as if bidding them a good day.

The scene from his point of view looked just like one of those picture postcards you could buy at interstate truck stops or one of the many gas station gift shops along I-85, the ones that always had something hollow and stupid written on them, like "Wish you were here," or "Greetings from the Sunny South!" When he reached his destination and went about his business, the view would be very different but right now, the scene was cheerful and welcoming, like something the city's chamber of commerce had ordered up to entice visitors to come here and spend a chunk of their hard-earned money.

Taking one more glance at the bustling town square, he shifted the Gran Torino into DRIVE, and turned right onto a side street, leaving the county courthouse in his rearview mirror. A sharp left down a narrow alleyway, then another left into the gravel parking lot, and he had arrived at his destination. He knew this little town like the back of his hand by now; he had staked out the area weeks before and had even made a couple of trial runs from his hotel to the Lawrenceville square. He had done his homework to make sure both the timing and the location were perfect. Now, it was show time.

Turning and reaching into the back floorboard of the car, he grabbed the day's tool of choice, which he had wrapped carefully in a white pillowcase. The .44 Marlin rifle felt heavy and solid in his hands, the weight of it both calming and exciting. A thin film of sweat now glistened on his brow, and small but growing wet stains dotted the fabric under his arms; in just a few minutes, the flannel would be damp and clinging to his body despite the day's near-perfect weather. That familiar quickening of his pulse, the rush of blood and adrenaline, were spiraling up now. It was always the same, and it was damn near better than sex for him. He'd never tire of the rush of stalking, then ultimately eliminating, his prey. Today, he planned to bag a big one.

An onlooker who might have happened upon the scene in the parking lot that day would probably not have remembered seeing a man there at all. There was certainly nothing unusual to see, nothing in particular that might later spark a memory. He was very good at becoming invisible; he had perfected the art of moving behind the scenery on the stage of reality a long time ago. He was alive today because he was a ghost when he chose to be. Though not even thirty years old, he was very good at what he did.

Glancing in the rearview mirror and to both sides of the dusty car, he opened the driver's side door and slipped out, careful to turn the rifle sideways as he did. He closed the door behind him, making sure to leave it unlocked. Every second would count once he accomplished what he came here to do.

He took just three or four long strides to get to the back steps of the building, then took the concrete steps two at a time. Leaning against the back door with his right shoulder, he threw his weight against the wood and for a split second, he felt the door resist. Mustering all of his effort, he once again hit the weathered door with his right shoulder. This time, it gave way so easily he nearly tumbled and landed headfirst on the dusty wood floor inside. Confusion, then doubt, threatened to take hold. A lesser man might have panicked, but not him. This was not his first rodeo. *The wood chock must have gotten wedged in too tight, that's all. Nobody's been in here and moved it.* He squinted and adjusted his glasses, studying the gray dust on the floor anyway, some of it lazily settling back onto the uneven boards after puffing up into the sunlight. The dirt was both glittery and chalky.

He was checking for footprints that didn't look like his, scrambling to find evidence to back up what he had just told himself. *Nobody's been in here for a while 'cept me.*

"Adidas brand athletic shoes," the forensics report would eventually disclose after the cops had analyzed the shoe prints both inside and outside the building, but it would take weeks for that to be discovered and even longer for cops to use it. He would be long gone well before then, vanishing like the misty vapor he had become. It was one of the things that frustrated the FBI most about him.

There were no other shoe prints in the fine gray dust on the floor. His hiding place was still secret, belonging only to him.

Four days ago, on his last scouting trip into this pissant little town, he had pried open the locked back door to the vacant building, then placed a thin piece of wood between the door and the jamb to be sure he could get in and get out quickly. Once he had gained his balance and was satisfied that no one had discovered his hiding place, he carefully closed the back door again, shoving the thin piece of wood back into place. He'd only be exiting this way one more time, and it would have to be quick, just like he'd practiced.

The shuffle of his footprints echoed off the bare floors and walls as he walked across the room toward the front door of what the locals called the "old rock building." The façade of the structure was made of flat rocks that had been pieced together, so he guessed that's where the name came from. A greenish-brown burlap curtain, held up by shiny new thumbtacks, still hung over the dirty glass of the front door. The window covering had been a last-minute idea of his, and a good one. One thing he had learned about these small towns was that everybody minded everybody else's business. Over the years, he had learned to be invisible, to fade into the scenery like a ghost, and an unremarkable one at that: there, but not quite. He had no intentions of having some old busybody spot his movements in what was supposed to be a deserted building, then calling the cops to report it. It was always the old ones you had to worry about, the ones who had nothing better to do than mind everyone else's business. Still, Joe Franklin (or James Vaughan or James Cooper, take your pick) had eluded both state and federal law enforcement with very little difficulty for years now. When they would ask witnesses whether they had seen anyone unusual hanging around a crime scene, or whether they had heard anything out of the ordinary, the answer was always the same: "No." That was just one of the reasons he knew he was doing the work of a God who loved white righteousness and hated niggers and Jews. He was doing the work of God, the same kind of work that God himself would do if he were walking around down here and saw, firsthand, the abominations that Joe committed.

Standing there by the front door of the abandoned building (his "sniper's nest" they would call it in the newspaper tomorrow, and he liked that a lot), he stepped to one side and pressed his back against the dirty, yellowed wall, feeling the coolness through his damp shirt. Careful not to make any sudden movements, he reached and pushed aside the burlap curtain he had tacked over the window. If he pressed his head back against the wall and looked to his right, he could see V&J Café right down the street. Directly across Perry Street was an old house in dire need of paint. Although it could have been abandoned, he knew better than to assume that. As it turned out, despite its rundown looks, the house right across the street was a group home. Squinting and adjusting his glasses, he peered intently at the windows of the house, looking for any movement at all. No, it wouldn't do to have any busybodies poking their nose into his dark business today.

After staring at the house for a minute or two, he didn't see anyone looking back at him. The house itself looked untidy, but the lawn looked as though it had been recently tended. Most of the houses situated on streets feeding the town square were as neat as a pin, with fresh paint and closely cropped lawns. The house across the way might have fooled a less experienced man. Right now anyway, it looked uninhabited. There was no one on the front porch. There was no movement in the windows. There were no cars parked in the cracked driveway.

A young mother walked into his line of sight, coming from the direction of the V&J. She was struggling to push a stroller while balancing some purchases she had made. She certainly was not paying attention to the abandoned rock building. She didn't notice the makeshift window covering on the front door. She had no way of knowing that a hate-fueled killer was watching her every step and that, even with some nasty work ahead of him, he was taking lustful inventory of what he saw. She was a little older than the women he preferred, girls really. But he liked the way she filled out the light pink sweater she was wearing. He liked the way her legs disappeared under the ever-so-tight skirt she wore, leaving just enough to the imagination of a secret admirer. He let his mind wander for a few seconds, then snapped back to the business at hand. The young mother would not know that, as she pushed her baby in a stroller along Perry Street, a man had watched her from the shadows, licking his lips and imagining what she looked like without her pink sweater and tweed skirt. Her husband would ask her later that day, as the anchor man on the six o'clock news read the sensational story of what had happened in Lawrenceville that day, whether she had noticed anything unusual in town. Of course, she would say that she did not. She wouldn't remember the chill that skittered down her spine when she walked north on Perry Street that afternoon, or the strange feeling that she couldn't seem to shake, as if someone was watching her. They never did.

He turned his attention back to the interior of the building. Leaning his rifle (still sound asleep inside the white pillowcase) against the dirty plaster wall, he walked across the bare planks toward the stairs that led to the second floor. He had about twenty minutes to kill, so he thought it best to double-check the upstairs, just to be safe. His footsteps echoed and bounced off the walls of the empty room, even though he walked softly. He felt that he was alone, but he had done this enough to know that he should make sure of it. *No room for mistakes. This one's too important.*

"It was carelessness killed the cat, not curiosity," he could hear his mother screeching as she dragged him across the cracked and lumpy linoleum floor of his childhood home, and he visibly winced at the mere memory of the raspy voice he hated so much.

He reached the foot of the stairs and paused, looking up into the dark stairwell, holding his breath and listening for any sound of movement. All he heard was silence, save for the ungraceful backfiring of a clumsy box truck somewhere nearby. He liked the sudden cracking sound, even though it made him jump. He liked it because it sounded an awful lot like a gunshot. A manufacturing plant located not too far from here gave up a similar sound every now and then, when a slow, deliberate crane would drop a bundle of wooden pallets from a height of about twenty feet. The crane would swing a bundle of pallets into place, the operator would push the control lever from left to right, and a thousand pounds or so of wood would crash down onto the gravel below, splitting the mornings or afternoons wide open with a loud "crack-crack!" The locals were so used to hearing those sounds that they rarely looked up from their desks, to see where it came from. Those sounds were his allies when he was on one of his missions. Misdirection and confusion are the hunter's friends.

The narrow stairs inside the building sounded hollow as he took them one at a time, his shoes scuffing through the dust and grit, whispering a terrible secret to each other that only he could hear. Reaching the top, he stopped for a moment, listening again for movement. Silence. Moving stealthily down the hallway, he nudged open creaky doors and checked behind them. In one room, there was an overstuffed chair leaning drunkenly on three legs; in another, an old work boot with a long-abandoned mouse nest built snugly inside it. A forgotten jacket hung in the closet of one room; an old toaster oven waited patiently for its next meal atop a dusty bureau in another. Two mice, long dead in traps that had snapped shut years ago, stood watch in the corner of the next room. In that same room, an old mattress, covered with cotton ticking and coughing up most of its stuffing onto the floor, was littered with used condoms. Liquor and beer bottles were scattered carelessly on the floor around it, but none of them looked like they had been left here recently.

His mind strayed again. Closing his eyes and licking his lips, he imagined young lovers sneaking in here and fucking in secret, sweating with urgency. He felt the familiar physical reaction to his imagination and swallowing hard, willed the dirty thoughts away as he had done so many times before. There was work to do.

Every upstairs room in the old building featured a single porcelain sink hanging on one wall, some of them hanging at crazy angles, caked with rust and dirt. Over the sinks perched dirty rectangular mirrors, black veining just underneath the surface, that marbling that gives one's reflection an other-worldly look, as if a ghost is looking back, lurking just under the glass.

The old rock building had once been a boarding house. As roomers had moved in and out over the years, they had left behind small clues as to who they were: a crumpled pay stub, an empty cologne bottle, a moth-eaten work shirt. In the first room he checked, there was an old black and white photograph of a man standing next to a woman who was holding a small child; the writing on the back was faded and illegible, but the date stamped in the margin was 1968. There were a lot of stories in these rooms, but none that interested him. Not today. *I'll leave my own mark on this rundown rat hole in this shit kickin' town. And when they find it, I'll be long gone.*

Having checked all but one of the upstairs rooms, he was nearly satisfied that he was in this place alone. Standing at the doorway of the very last room on the left, he eased the door open and checked for any sign of recent activity. There was none. Walking over to the window that faced the town square, he stopped briefly to examine his reflection in the mandatory mirror hung over the mandatory white sink. The man that looked back at him was slender and tightly muscled. His hair, thinning in spots from frequent dye and bleach jobs, stuck to his forehead in wet clumps. His wire-rimmed glasses sat slightly askew. Absentmindedly, he straightened them and walked over to the window that faced the center of town. Hiding in the shadows, not daring to use his elbow to wipe the grimy glass, he squinted and peered, one more time, down onto the busy square one block over.

Cars sat in rows along the streets, waiting patiently for a green light and their turn to go. The townspeople, no doubt the area's movers and shakers, were industriously going about their business. Lawrenceville is the county seat for Gwinnett County, Georgia, and as such, all the county's business and some of the state's business were conducted right here in this picturesque little municipality. The politicians and lawyers gathered here five days a week to conduct the business of screwing their fellow man as thoroughly and as efficiently as possible. He had nothing but contempt for all of them, but he would not be distracted. They were not the reason he was here today, either. They were not his concern. He was here today, holed up in this dusty, vacant rooming house looking for one man, and one man only. He was here today to topple another domino (a big one), to incite an uprising among the nation's whites that had been a long time coming. It was high time to take back the country, and he would show them the way.

CHAPTER 4
The Letter
(1983)

Detective Michael Cowart

But my apologies. My opinions about the story I am about to tell are not important. Still, when a man has spent his life seeking truth and justice, it is difficult not to paint the memories with his own colors. I find myself reminiscing more than I ought these days, I suppose. While that is not normally true, recently it has been. Ever since I read a recent newspaper article about a case I had worked years ago as a law enforcement officer, I find myself thinking about books that I believed had been closed long ago, never to be reopened.

Now back to the subject of my first encounter with Joseph Paul Franklin. On a late summer day about thirty years ago, I sat at my desk, pondering a letter that I had opened and read, it seemed, for the hundredth time. The letter was dated August 5, 1983. It was from Joseph P. Franklin, inmate number 01517–018, Federal Penitentiary, Marion, Illinois, via his then attorney J. Frank Kimbrough. It was adressed to Gwinnett County PD chief John Crunkleton, my boss. I had no way of knowing this at the time, but I would later learn that Joe Franklin refused to deal with Gwinnett District Attorney Bryant Huff because he was, in Franklin's mind, a "Jew." Now as far as I know, DA Huff was a Methodist or a Baptist or something along those lines. All I know is that he wasn't Jewish. But if Franklin said you were a Jew, then in his mind, you were a Jew. I would also come to learn that there was no rhyme or reason to his rationale, but there it was, just the same.

The letter read, simply, "I would like to know if you could do me a favor. Would you write a letter to (Chief Crunkleton) and advise him that I am currently incarcerated at the Federal Penitentiary at Marion, Illinois, and would like to know if he would send an investigator up here to talk to me, as I have knowledge of a case in which he may be interested. Thanks."

The brief note had been officially received by the department as evidence, the red stamp at the bottom of the page bright and official. *Evidence, yes, but of what, exactly?* I wondered. Leaning back in my government-issued office chair and running both hands through my hair (a habit I developed years ago, according to my wife, when I was trying to reduce a complex problem to a simple one), I read the brief missive again.

Crunkleton passed the letter on to me because at the time, I was his Administrative Aide. Franklin's offer to share knowledge about a case in which we'd be interested could turn out to be a bonanza, or it could fizzle like a wet firecracker. It was my job to figure out where this was going.

"I have knowledge of a case in which he may be interested." Rolling those words around in my head, I thought *Could it be?* I didn't dare hope, but it's the only case that came to mind. I had heard rumblings from other law enforcement agencies, and I had read reports and alerts issued by the FBI that hinted at a connection to an unsolved shooting case here in the county seat, but I hadn't really believed that anything would come of the insistent buzz about this elusive man.

Five years earlier, the publisher of *Hustler* magazine, Larry Flynt, was shot in Gwinnett County while on trial for a state misdemeanor obscenity charge. One of his attorneys, local criminal defense attorney Gene Reeves, was also shot in the same incident. The shooter had never been caught. There had never been any leads that panned out, never any credible eyewitnesses, and certainly not the benefit of a confession from anyone. It was as if a ghost had come to our town square, shot the two men, then vanished into thin air. I had read at one time, probably about three years ago, that the FBI boys had drawn a tentative connection between Franklin and the shooting but to my knowledge, there was nothing more than suspicion on the table.

I guess you could say that Franklin had our attention at that point, but there's something that battle-savvy detectives and investigators know about prisoners offering information, and that is that there is always a price for that information. There truly is no honor among thieves, and I've had many a conversation with cunning criminals who would sell their own mother if it meant that doing so would shave a few measly months off of a lengthy prison sentence. It is always best to proceed with caution, and with a grain of salt, when an inmate offers up information.

That short, concise letter from Franklin prompted a response from Crunkleton the day after he received it, and on August 15, he fired off a letter to H. G. Miller, Warden of the US Penitentiary in Marion. Crunkleton made it clear to Miller that yes, his investigators would very much like to talk to Franklin about the case in question, and they'd like to do so as soon as possible.

Franklin was serving two consecutive life sentences in the Marion prison for killing two black joggers in Utah and an interracial couple in Wisconsin. He was in Marion simply because it was the highest security federal prison in the United States at the time, and he was a tricky character. In fact, inside Marion, he and a handful of other inmates were housed in a special holding area. Even in a super-max prison, Franklin was treated like an escape threat, because he was. He had escaped custody twice before, in two different states, and there would not be a third time. Not from Marion, anyway.

I learned from Franklin, through a few more letters and a couple of phone conversations, that he hated living in that super maximum security prison in Illinois. He wanted out, and he was willing to do whatever it took (so he said) to make that happen. As a Marion inmate, Franklin was never allowed to go outside. He was allowed less than an hour a day in a very small enclosure outside his cell. The area was open to the sky but surrounded by high, thick concrete walls. The opening, well above Franklin's reach, was covered with wire. From inside that enclosure, he could see a tiny slice of the sky that looked as though it had been pieced together like one of those 500-piece puzzles, because of the wire that covered the opening.

That was it, the sum total of his outdoor experience since he'd been at Marion. That small, faraway opening covered with wire was the only means Franklin had of knowing whether it was sunny, cloudy, or rainy outside. He hadn't felt the outside temperature in years. He was a runner, as the guards at Marion and other prisons referred to him and any other prisoners who had a hard time staying put. He was a runner, and they would not give him an opportunity to run anywhere at Marion.

A Cincinnati law enforcement conference designed for information sharing between states (remember that back then, there was no national database), had uncovered patterns in recent crimes that had placed Franklin high on a list of suspects in several shootings, some bombings, and many bank robberies. The wide-scoped investigation revealed the fact that Franklin was the chief suspect in the May 29, 1980 shooting of Atlanta attorney and Civil Rights leader Vernon Jordan. His *modus operandi* was becoming consistently evident in comparisons of several shootings, including the one in Gwinnett County, as I had mentioned before. In fact, he was beginning to look very much like a serial killer.

After Franklin had made that initial contact with our office through his attorney, Chief Crunkleton, "Mac" McKelvey, and I worked with Warden Miller and his staff to arrange a face-to-face meeting with him. Such a meeting would be the true litmus test;

was he offering valuable information, even a confession? Or was he working us like he had so cleverly worked the officers from whom he escaped in Florence, Kentucky?

An observant police officer in Florence, Kentucky noticed a gun on the back seat of Franklin's car when it was parked on the street one afternoon. A records check revealed that the owner of the car, a James Cooper, had an outstanding warrant for car theft, so the officer waited for him to return to the car, then arrested him, charging him with the car theft. He was also being held for further questioning by the FBI in the Kentucky jail, based on additional information that the officers received after Franklin's arrest. This may come as a surprise, but Joe Franklin, as is true of many psycho- or sociopaths, could be very charming when he wanted to be. He could carry on delightful conversation, when doing so served his purposes. That is exactly how Franklin escaped from the Florence, Kentucky jail, right under the noses of several police officers.

At any rate, the FBI had distributed his photograph to blood banks all over the southeast, since giving blood provided him with backup income if it had been a while since he robbed a bank. This fact, this seemingly innocent tidbit of knowledge about Joseph Franklin, would prove to be his undoing.

We knew that we were dealing with both an extremist and a clever opportunist. His second escape was actually from a Utah courthouse during the penalty phase of another murder trial in Salt Lake City. He was recaptured within hours, on another floor of the courthouse, but he had proven to law enforcement agents at all levels that if he could escape, he would.

Why was he reaching out to us now? I believe now there were several reasons, but at the top of that list was the fact that he wanted out of the Marion prison. The conditions in which he was forced to live were, in his own words, "cruel and inhumane."

In the warden's opinion, as well as the opinions of any judges or panels who had knowledge of the special security measures for

Franklin, he had earned that strict treatment by escaping custody twice before, but he didn't see it that way. In my experience, they never did. I don't believe I ever interviewed an offender who thought he was being treated fairly by the justice system or by the prison in which he lived.

CHAPTER 5
The Alabama Soil
(1950s and 1960s)

MOBILE, ALABAMA, IN the early 1960s was a town in the painful throes of change. Buried deep in the southern United States, Alabama and her sister states had for many years depended heavily on the land for a living; cotton was the primary form of agriculture that had propped up the Southern economy in the 1800s, and with the labor-intensive cotton plantations came indentured servitude. Slaves. The cotton and slave industries in the Deep South were both lucrative and conjoined; without one, there could not be the other.

In the 1960s, Mobile was not as far removed from the dark era of slavery as history has been rewritten to imply. The ignorance and poverty that slavery left in its wake did not dissipate overnight, or in a few years, or even within an entire generation. The hate that had been bred into young black children, and the disdain that had been bred into young white children, were alive and well in the South even fifty years ago. Of course, the buying and selling of humans had been outlawed as a result of the Civil War and the signing of the Thirteenth Amendment in December 1865, but hate, even a hundred years later, still hung heavy in the air like the biting smell of gunpowder and the sickeningly sweet smell of decay, like the smell of death, and like the spilled blood of generations.

The young boy, known around here as Jimmy to most, James Clayton to his mama, sat hidden under the broken down porch, gravel digging into his backside and an occasional mouse skittering across his too-small work boots. Occasionally, a tail or some twitching whiskers flirted into the holes on the bottoms of his shoes, and the boy would absently kick them away. The mice didn't scare him, mind you. He just kicked at them when they were toying with the idea of climbing inside one of those holes.

The dank air, heavy with humidity and the smell of fresh-cut grass from out on the highway, was both suffocating and soothing at the same time. He drew in a deep breath of it, filling his lungs, then exhaled slowly and quietly so as not to give away his hiding place. If she found him crouched out here under the porch, he really believed she might actually, finally, kill him. The boy couldn't remember the last time he woke up and didn't fear, deep down in his belly, that today would be the day his mother would just go on and kill him, and get it over with. Jimmy Vaughn, Jr., had lived with that fear for as long as he could remember, for almost every day of his twelve long years on earth.

His daddy had left the family a couple of years ago. He'd just up and left, with no explanation, no note, no reason that Jimmy or his brother and sisters could figure on their own. The second oldest of the four Vaughn siblings, Jimmy couldn't see that his father's leaving mattered that much anyway. The only real difference he had seen since James Sr. just walked out and never looked back was that he wasn't yelling or hitting his children all day, and passed out on the sofa at night. Mama wasn't calling the cops on him two or three times a week when he got out of hand, the stench of cheap liquor on his breath. Jimmy had heard talk around town that the war had messed his daddy up real bad. He guessed it was so.

Mama never talked about it, either. Helen Rau Vaughn was a woman of few words. The daughter of immigrant Germans, her preferred methods of expressing her feelings were via a stiff upper lip and a mean kick or a slap upside the head. She loved to express herself to her kids, mainly Jimmy, every chance she got.

The boy leaned back against the cool concrete wall under the porch and closed his eyes. Instinctively, he reached into his back pocket to feel for his book. It was still there. Just touching it calmed him, and he relaxed against the wall again, taking comfort in the solid, cool feel of it. He wished he could live here sometimes, just live right here under this porch all by himself. The light was usually good enough to read by, and this was the only place in which he felt alone and safe. He liked the feeling of both. He wasn't even scared to sleep out here at night. He had done that a few times, when things had gotten so bad that he thought his mama really might kill him, or hurt him real bad.

It was always the same; something would set her off, and he would be the one to pay the price for it. If it was a really bad day, she would even beat his brother and his sisters, but the brunt of her anger always seemed to land square on Jimmy's shoulders. His mother hated him, and he had no idea why. As a child, she had been abused by her mother ("Mort," she used to call her, but no one was quite sure why), so he supposed she just didn't know any better. He had overheard her telling a story to his father one time, during one of the infrequent, explosive visits the patriarch paid his family, about how one time Mort was beating her so bad and she was crying and yelling so loud that Mort shoved a rag clear down her throat to shut her up. It nearly choked her to death, but the beating didn't stop. In her rigid, stoic manner, she told that story just as calm and even as if she was talking about the weather, to somebody she met in the market. It didn't take nothing to set her off when it came to her kids, but she could tell this awful story as though it didn't matter to her one bit.

A waitress trying in vain to support four children, Helen Vaughn had endured many a beating at the hands of her husband, an epileptic and a shattered alcoholic who had left the family high and dry after he came home from World War II, "the big one," as his father often referred to it. James Sr. was a butcher by trade (later on in life, Jimmy would appreciate the irony of that), but he was really an alcoholic by trade after the war. Something bad had happened to him over there. Jimmy couldn't imagine what it was, but it had messed him up, all right. Daddy would come back to visit from time to time, often going a few years between appearances, but the occasions were never happy ones when he did show up. When he wasn't drunk, he was either violent or working himself up to getting that way. Her husband's "visits" always left Helen with just one more reason to be angry.

The cool bumpiness of the concrete against his back felt good. It soothed him. He loved it under here. No, it would not do for her to find him here. It was his one safe spot, where he could think, doze, gobble whatever food he could scrounge without being caught, but most important of all, he could read. He wasn't real good at it, not yet anyway, but at the age of twelve, he liked to read. Even reading the kid stuff he could decipher, Jimmy Vaughn felt like reading took him away from here, away from this crappy old house, away from his cruel mother, and away from the kids at school who bullied him incessantly, especially after he had to get glasses. A nasty tumble off of his bike that same year had left his right eye damaged, nearly completely blind. For some reason, his damaged eye and the fact that he wore thick glasses as a result had really gotten the attention of the school bullies, the ones who picked on every kid at school except the ones in their own mean and hateful group. Rarely a school day went by that Jimmy Vaughn didn't have to try to bicycle past his torturers, just to get the living shit beat out of him for his trouble.

Reading plucked the tormented young boy right up out of hot and sticky Mobile and took him wherever he wanted to go. Yes, he loved it under here.

"James Clayton Vaughn? Where the hell are you, you worthless little bastard? I told you not to go runnin' off. You just wait, boy. You just wait til I get my hands on you!" His mother's screaming jolted him out of his peaceful reverie; his heart slammed against the walls of his chest as if to warn him of impending danger. She had banged the ailing screen door shut after shouting for him at the top of her lungs. The door had hung at an awkward and useless angle ever since the last time she had one of her spells (that's what she called it when she beat the hell out of him for no apparent reason—a "spell"). The popping and screeching noise it made as she slammed it shut this time punctuated the last of her ominous threat; Jimmy was sure she had done that intentionally. Oh, how he hated her. When she would shout, "You just wait!" it meant bad news for him, he could bet on that. He held his breath and didn't dare move, even to shoo away the grayish-brown mouse that had scrambled up and perched inquisitively on his boot. It stared at him as if to say, "Well, your mother's looking for you. Aren't you going to answer her, you worthless little bastard?"

He slowly exhaled, shifting slightly to move his hand away from the rotted latticework that had, at one time, been a decorative addition to the crappy back porch attached to the rear of the crappy house in this crappy government-assisted neighborhood. He moved his hand out of the sliver of sunlight that had crept into his hiding place, because if she saw him right now, it would be bad for him. He knew that much.

The mouse continued to nibble on the crumb it had found, probably one that had fallen off his sausage biscuit when he had scurried under here earlier. *How much earlier, though. Isn't that the question?* It tilted its gray-brown head and peered at him, nervously chewing the morsel it had found next to the boy when he had been asleep. "Well, you'd better answer her, or she's going to beat the hell out of you when she finds you," the mouse seemed to say as it masticated its tiny morsel.

She had left a plate of biscuits on the stove this morning, and he had pilfered one on the way out the door, careful to rearrange the rest of them so that she wouldn't notice right away. Mama was as stingy with food as she was with affection—another German trait, his daddy used to say. By the time he was twelve years old, Jimmy Vaughn was twenty pounds less than, and developmentally about three years behind, his peers.

The screen door right above his head creaked open again, and then slammed reluctantly shut amid screeches and gratings of protest; the sound startled Jimmy so badly he peed his pants, right there in the dirt and gravel under the porch. The mouse tilted its furry little head and Jimmy could have sworn that it seemed to be grinning at him. The boy and the small creature sat there for (*a minute? an hour?*), just looking at one another, as if each was waiting for the other to make a move.

Without warning and in one swift movement, Jimmy grabbed the piece of splintered, rotting wood in the dirt near his right hand and smashed that damned mouse flat, right there on his boot. The mouse never knew what hit it, the boy's effort was so quick and deliberate. After he had done it, Jimmy Vaughn just sat there and stared at his feet and the mess that covered his shoes and the hem of his pants. Oh, that would cost him all right. She'd be furious when she saw that. *Did I do that?* In a very deep and secret place in the pit of his belly, the thought terrified him, because he already knew the answer. *Did I really do that? I must have.*

His face streaked with sweat and tears, Jimmy sat there under the ramshackle back porch that was practically falling off the house in which he had lived his entire miserable life. He sat there for a very long time.

When he opened his eyes again, he was still leaning against the cool concrete wall. The rough texture of the wall was real. It was solid, and it was real, and as always, it comforted him. Reaching around to his back pocket, he felt for his book; feeling it was there, he was calmed, reassured. Hair and dirt clung to the back of his neck in sweaty clumps, and he stunk to high heavens. His stomach rolled; the boy felt ill, like he might vomit. Mockingbirds and sparrows were bickering back and forth in the trees separating his mother's house from the neighbors. The late afternoon sun was reaching in between the slats of the rotted lattice, trying to clutch at his hand; his shirt was sticky with sweat. Mosquitoes were swarming and buzzing, feasting on the exposed skin of his face, hands, and ankles.

His pants were wet down there, but just barely. *How long have I been under here?* He couldn't be sure, but his growling stomach hinted that it had been at least two hours, maybe even three. In his hand, he held a piece of wood, cracked nearly in half and smeared with blood and fur. He looked at it in confused terror. *What happened? Where did that come from?* His palm was gouged and tender, with several large splinters embedded deep under the dirty skin. His knuckles were bloodied. All he could think of when he looked at his boots was how angry his mother would be when she saw the mess on them. She didn't like buying her children clothes even when they had outgrown the old ones; she sure wasn't going to be happy to see that he had ruined his shoes by—*By doing what? What happened to my shoes? Is that blood?* The limp and lifeless ball of sticky, matted fur in the dirt answered his question. The dead mouse, or what was left of it, lay there accusing him. *He didn't even get to finish eating his crumb.* And for some reason, that one thought was the thought that disturbed Jimmy the most. He had smashed the inquisitive mouse before it had the chance to finish its purloined snack. Before he could stop himself, the boy began to sob with broken abandon. His breath hitched in his chest as he brayed and bawled like a sobbing little girl. *Please, please stop. She'll hear you.* But his sobs were uncontrollable now. All he could do was let them come.

For the first time in the young man's life, he feared something other than his parents. These periods of blank blackness, of losing track of time, scared him every bit as much as Helen and James Vaughn Sr. did. As much as the thick, mean bullies who delighted in torturing him. Maybe a little bit more.

Daylight was waning, and the mosquitoes swarmed and buzzed around his face in a thick, hungry cloud. The oak tree in the neighbors' yard no longer threw its shadow across the lawn (if you could call the dusty, hard patch of dried clay a lawn). Lightning bugs played hide-and-seek around and under the porch; the gnats and ants had discovered the delectable treat smeared all over Jimmy's boots, and they were gorging themselves on the feast. He blinked, fighting to push down the dazed confusion that threatened the safety of his hiding place. *How long this time?* He swiped at his face, but it was dry. The tears had long since turned to streaks of sticky salt. Beside him, his book lay in the dirt, and the back cover and spine were smeared with blood. Part of the cover was torn off, the tiny piece of paper nowhere in sight. *How did that happen?* He picked up the book and wiped the mostly-dried blood off of it, carefully and thoughtfully. Not all of it would come off, and he again found himself crying uncontrollably, spittle and snot dripping out of his mouth and nose onto the book, making the mess even worse. His head began pounding like a bass drum, and the edges of his vision were turning gray again, like he was looking through a keyhole. In just a minute, if this episode was to be like any of the others he'd been experiencing since the accident, he would lose consciousness and wake up having done God knows what, God knows where. The thought made him sick to his stomach and this time, he did vomit down the front of his shirt and onto the bloody, pee-smelling clay between his legs. Something was wrong with him, of that he was sure. Sometimes, after one of these episodes, the only way he could piece together events was to backtrack over the day and try to fill in the blanks.

He had been sitting at the kitchen table by himself, eating a sausage biscuit, the grease from the cold meat congealed and slick on the roof of his mouth. His siblings had already eaten; he was late getting to the table because Mama had sent him up to the store to get her some cigarettes. When he returned, he opened the reluctant screen door with one hand, careful not to bring attention to his return from his errand. He had gotten to looking at the new comic books they had got in down at the drugstore, and lost all track of time.

The house was quiet, save for the ticking of the Pepsi-Cola clock over the stove, and the tinny chatter of a radio from somewhere upstairs. Jimmy tiptoed across the warped linoleum, looked over his shoulder toward the living room, then selected a sausage biscuit from the few that were left on the plate on the counter. Tiptoeing to the table, he carefully slid a chair out and slipped quietly into it. Thoughtfully chewing his breakfast, his mind wandered to maybe sneaking off to the fishing hole this afternoon, after his chores were done. Lost in his reverie, he began tapping his foot on the worn linoleum to the beat of Merle Haggard's "Okie from Muskogee," the song that was now floating through the house from the upstairs bedroom.

And just like that, out of the blue and for no reason at all, Mama came up behind him and slapped him so hard it made his ears ring. "Sit up straight while you're at my table! And where the hell are my cigarettes, you lazy good-for-nothing?" she shrieked. Before he could answer, she stomped over to the kitchen counter, snatched the pack up, and jammed it into the pocket of her apron. She left the room as suddenly as she had entered it. Jimmy sat up straight, ears ringing and tears stinging his eyes. *I hate her. I wish I could kill her.* She seemed to hate everybody in that house. She seemed to need to attack and fight everyone, but she saved a special hatred for her oldest son.

Daddy had always explained her behavior away, blaming it on the fact that her mother had beat her, and now she felt it was her job to beat her kids. To tell the truth, she actually seemed to enjoy it. That didn't make any sense to Jimmy, already withdrawn and socially trailing other kids his age. The Vaughn children were rarely allowed to play with other children, so as far as they knew, what went on in their home was normal. Only it wasn't, and no one knew that better than Jimmy. *If somebody beat on you when you was a kid, why would you want to beat on your own kids? That don't make sense.*

He sat at the table and finished his breakfast, making sure his shoulders were squared and his feet planted firmly underneath the table, just in case she came back. Of course if she did, it wouldn't matter how straight and still he sat. She'd just find something else to surprise him with, some other infraction that would give her cause to scream at him and give him the backside of her hand.

He remembered finishing the first biscuit and grabbing another as he sneaked out the back door. He took the back steps two at a time; making sure he wasn't being observed from any of the windows on this side of the house, he jiggled a piece of rotten porch lattice loose and slid it to one side. Darting underneath the porch, he replaced the lattice exactly the way it was, then duck-walked to the far end of the dark, cool area underneath. Scooting his feet outward, he leaned backward until the cool, rough wall touched his back. It took a while for him to settle down, for the peace to overtake the rage that even now was building inside him.

Try as he might, Jimmy Vaughn could not recall the rest of the afternoon that day, not all of it, anyway. The knots in his stomach pulled tighter, hardening into a ball, at the sound of his mother's voice coming from directly above him. For a split second, he allowed himself to daydream. He imagined himself scratching on all fours out from the dirt under the porch, springing up the dilapidated steps, and beating his mother to death with a baseball bat. The thought of that actually made him smile. That would shut her up.

He didn't dare move, for fear of giving away one of his last remaining hideaways. Sure enough, she had come out just for a moment, then gone back inside, stomping, screaming, and slamming doors as she went. No doubt she was now going from room to room in the house uttering the same demand for her son, her wrath building with every step she took. He'd sure have to stay out of her way now, even though he'd pay the price for avoiding her later on.

The sound of raindrops pattering on the leaves and debris just the other side of the dirty lattice had begun, and far off in the distance, thunder rumbled.

As the sunlight faded and the crickets got to talking to one another, Jimmy Vaughn curled himself up into a ball and fell asleep, right there in the dirt under the porch. His dreams were filled with fear and vengeance and hate, but he slept just the same.

CHAPTER 6
Inside the Belly of the Beast
(1983)

Detective Michael Cowart

"Well, look at this map. See anything familiar?" I threw a haphazardly folded map into my co-pilot's lap, grinning and winking at him as I did so.

I was flying the twin engine Cessna on the way to southern Illinois; Mac and Tony Lowe (Tony was the police aviation unit commander for Gwinnett) were my passengers, and Mac was sitting in the back seat, dozing off and on.

"I don't, Mike. We're off course. We have to be," Lowe answered.

"Look out the window then. Anything?" I asked, with poorly controlled panic in my voice. In feigned desperation, I threw a map book to Mac. "Look at that and tell me, are we on course? Do you see anything at all that looks familiar?"

Now Mac had an extensive vocabulary. It was one of the things among many I had always admired about the man. While he never blasphemed, I believe he used every word in that impressive vocabulary as he let us both know what he thought of our little prank. Of course we knew exactly where we were; we were on a direct course to arrive in Marion not just on time, but a few minutes early. The fake panic and pretense of being lost was just one of our little jokes that lightened what were usually some very tense situations. We all had a laugh when Mac was finished telling us what he thought about our hoax, and the rest of the flight was spent mostly in silence.

It was September 16, a beautiful day. The views down below were stunning, as well; blue-green squares of pasture and farmland in Kentucky, rippling cornfields in Illinois. When I flew low enough over Kentucky, we caught glimpses here and there of majestic and very expensive horses, and the multi-million-dollar farms on which they lived.

It had been about a month since we had received Franklin's letter offering information about a case, and now we were going to see just what he had to say. By now, we were sure that he had been referring to the March 1978 shooting of Larry Flynt and Gene Reeves. His attorney had confirmed that for us, though he himself denied having any knowledge of the case or circumstances surrounding it. Attorneys. You had to love them, though in Kimbrough's case, I believed him. Franklin changed attorneys as often as most of us changed our socks. Kimbrough probably knew less about his client than we did, as he was just one in a long line of Franklin's hired and fired lawyers.

There was no question that we were going to meet with him to talk about what he knew about some pretty dark deeds he'd committed, both in Georgia and in other states. We still didn't know for sure what he wanted in return for this information, but we had a pretty good idea. My guess was that he wanted to be transferred out of Marion prison. Not only was the security tight and virtually infallible, but also Franklin truly believed that he was the victim of a conspiracy. He was convinced that Warden Miller was "a Jew," and that the entire place was run by "niggers and Jews." With the very limited communication from Franklin that I had read at this point, I could already see that his views were both twisted and offensive. I was even then beginning to understand that Joseph Franklin was very capable of committing the crimes of which the FBI suspected him.

The super-max prison in Marion, Illinois, was not a pleasant place to be in the mid-1980s. It is a severe-looking gray compound surrounded by several live chain fence perimeters and rivers of wickedly jagged razor wire. By 1978, it was near the top of the list of the country's highest security prisons, a state-of-the-art masterpiece. Designed to house only the worst of the worst offenders (many who called Marion "home" were transfers from the infamous and now defunct Alcatraz prison), inmates spent at least twenty-three hours every day alone in their cells.

Despite the prison's stringent security guidelines, in 1983 guards Merle Clutts and Robert Hoffman were murdered by inmates, in separate well-planned incidents that took place only hours apart. The warden's reaction was swift and severe; as I remember thinking then and even now, it should have been. Sadly, there are some people in this world that understand nothing but harsh severity. I have met my fair share of them.

Miller placed the prison on permanent lockdown after those two guards were killed; Marion went from being a prison with pretty tight security procedures to being one of the tightest security "super max" penitentiaries in the country. One area of Marion had been converted to a control unit prison, home to inmates who would likely never step outside again. The control unit housed high-escape-risk prisoners as well as the most ruthless and infamous offenders in the United States. Also called "the belly of the beast" and "the end of the line" by her inmates and civil rights activists alike, Marion was typically reserved for the hardest of the hardcore offenders. Prisoners were not allowed to dine together, exercise together, or even practice religion in groups. In fact, after the two guards were murdered, recreation was limited to walking laps within one's cell. Punching bags, jump ropes, weights, and every other amenity in the recreation room had been removed, and permanently. Solitary confinement was the rule at Marion for every one of the nearly four hundred prisoners, which included such high-profile characters as mafia boss John Gotti, Christopher Boyce ("Falcon" of the Falcon and Snowman espionage duo), former CIA agent and spy Edwin Wilson, racketeering porn king Mike Thevis, and of course the man whom we were traveling to see, Joseph Paul Franklin. Security protocol at Marion, while criticized by some as being punitive, was simply a matter of safety.

We spent the rest of the flight in silence, partly because we were enjoying the brilliant views, but there was another reason, as well. No one inside the small plane had to put words to it; we had all been doing this long enough to understand what the others were thinking. Tony was along for the ride, so to speak. It was department protocol to have two licensed pilots on any plane that left the ground for department business. He understood the importance of this meeting, without a doubt. But Mac and I were both quietly apprehensive about our business on this trip. We had both been to other prisons, of course, most of them in Georgia. Just before we left for this trip, I myself had visited both Jackson (a diagnostic prison) and Reidsville (Georgia's main high security prison), and I assure you, both of those prisons are dark, gray, and oppressive to the point of suffocation. What always strikes me inside most prisons is the noise; guards and inmates bustle about incessantly, intent on completing whatever their mission of the moment is. I have often thought of that buzz as being "nervous boredom," too many men with too little to do. It's a lot like the sound of a pressure cooker building up steam. The echoes inside those walls multiply that noise to a point that the sounds are almost unbearable. I have to assume that both the guards and the inmates get accustomed to it over time. I don't know how else one would survive even a day without becoming numb to that awful, relentless noise. Thinking becomes nearly impossible, as it is drowned out by the cacophony of a normal day that unfolds inside those walls.

The only completely quiet place within a prison that I had ever visited was the room that held the electric chair at Jackson. It wasn't just quiet. It was silent. There's a difference, mind you. That room, the last room that some ruined men will ever see before drawing their final breath, is separate from the main building. That of course explains the "quiet"; the "silent," however, is another matter. There is something very solemn, very ominous, in the air inside a killing room. I cannot explain it any better than that. This room had just one purpose, and it was a dark one. The weight of that purpose was very real, and I felt it, just as surely as I would have felt a change in temperature or lighting.

When I was a much younger man, and being the habitual idiot I was back then, I volunteered to be strapped into that chair inside that room at Jackson Prison. I had heard other cops talk about having done the same thing, so of course I would not be outdone.

I was all right until the guard began strapping my head back against the chair. I told him that if he didn't stop, he might as well go ahead and throw the switch, because if I got out of that chair, I'd kill him on the spot. I can't think of another time in my life, or of anything else I had ever done, that was as deeply disturbing as being strapped into that chair. It was a feeling of absolute powerlessness, a deep-down knowledge that you could do nothing in that chair except take what was coming next. I have never been so glad to get out of a place as I was that chair, in that room, all those years ago.

Mac had had similar experiences, although I doubt he was ever reckless or stupid enough to allow someone to strap him into an electric chair. What I mean to say is that he had been inside prisons many times before, often with me, and he knew the same feelings and apprehensions that I just explained. We both expected Marion to be the same, or likely worse, than any facility we had ever visited before. It was built, after all, as a replacement for Alcatraz, and we knew that it housed some of the most devious, dangerous criminals in the country. We both expected a dark gray, stoic structure and most of all, I suppose, we were preparing ourselves for that God-awful, nerve-jangling noise that characterizes most prisons. Too many men, too little to do.

Of course, we were also thinking about that first face-to-face interview with Joseph Franklin. The meeting had to be productive, not just an idle wild goose chase. Without a doubt, there was a lot weighing on our minds on this trip. There was a lot at stake.

The drive to the Holiday Inn from the small airport was pleasant, as I remember. The endless cornfields, which had looked like square patches on a massive quilt from inside the Cessna, waved lazily in a late summer breeze. Mid-September in Illinois is much cooler than it is in Georgia, and I was glad that my dear wife had thought to send along a light jacket with me on this trip. The mere thought of my wife, so far away from this place and our purpose for being here, twisted inside my stomach, a pang that made me uncharacteristically homesick all of a sudden. We decided to head straight to the prison after stopping off at the hotel, simply because we wanted to take care of our business as quickly and as efficiently as possible. Yes, we wanted to be done—and quickly—but there was also an intricate and unbreakable succession of events that had to take place in order to talk with Franklin. The warden at Marion was very clear that arranging a face-to-face meeting with Joseph Franklin required rigid protocol, and that protocol would not be broken.

The approach to the prison at Marion marked an abrupt, jarring end to the pleasant drive and countryside vistas we had enjoyed on the trip from the airport. My first thought on seeing the prison was that they really meant business here.

Tall concrete machine gun guard towers, and row after row of barbed wire fences separated by waves of razor wire were the first things we saw on the grounds. We knew that we were close to our destination when the fields of corn gave way to sparse, patchy woods, then what seemed like miles of closely cropped green grass. The guard towers, fences, and razor wire were a harsh "hello," and even the occasional banter inside our car dried up when we got our first glimpse of Marion herself.

We parked our rental in the visitors' lot, noting that no matter which space we chose, we were always in full view of at least one guard tower. From here, we could better see the facility itself, with its imposing modern buildings and architecture. A strange thought sprinted through my mind as we got out of the car and quietly closed the doors, as if we were being careful not to wake the sleeping beast. Marion reminded me very much of the National Security Administration headquarters in Maryland, where I had spent so much of my time several lifetimes ago. Both places were very neat, very controlled, and very secure. And then another rogue thought: *Whether trying to keep someone in or someone out, the facilities look very much the same.*

Our first stop was at an outlying building on the grounds, the first layer of security. Here, a stoic, poker-faced guard verified our credentials and our appointment. If he knew who we were (and rest assured, he knew exactly who we were and why we were there), he didn't show it. After a call to security by the guard in this building, we were then on to the main building. I recall very clearly a strong sense of being watched with every step we took, and from more than one direction. At the end of that very long walk along that wide concrete walkway, we entered the main facility through glass doors that were so spotlessly clean they looked invisible.

The interior of the facility was impressively large. The floor was gleaming, white and gray tiles shined to mirror-like perfection. To our surprise, the air inside smelled fresh and clean, not stale and used as it does at the other prisons with which we were familiar. The biggest surprise though, to both Mac and me (Tony had stayed at the hotel; he was off the job until we flew back to Atlanta), was the deafening quiet. Marion prison was as quiet and still as a tightly-sealed tomb.

The buildings and grounds at the prison were maintained by inmate trustees, not from Marion prison, of course, but from a low-security work camp just a few miles down the road that had been established for just that purpose. Those prisoners were bused over in the mornings, worked all day, and then were transported back over to their facility at night. I can imagine that getting a close-up look at Marion was probably the best crime deterrent in the world. I can't imagine being inside that suffocating building and ever having a desire to live there. It was clean, yes, but it was also foreboding and oppressive.

Just inside the glass doors and to our right, I saw a U.S. Federal Courtroom, set up inside the prison to avoid the need to transport prisoners elsewhere for trials and hearings. To our left was a row of administrative offices. We saw no movement, heard no noises.

The main lobby floor sloped upward toward a central guard station; there was no question that that's where we were supposed to go now that we were inside. Once there, we went through the same screening process as before. Our IDs and credentials were verified, and the purpose of our visit was checked, then re-checked. Once we were cleared, a stern but polite deputy warden met us, briefing us on procedures and making very sure that we understood how this meeting would be hosted and conducted. He explained to us that the entire prison was on lockdown during our arrival and would be again when we left. In fact, hard lockdown would last four hours; therefore, our meeting with Franklin would last exactly four hours. The lockdown meant that every prisoner had to be sequestered securely in his cell, and every guard had to man his post for the entire length of our visit. Whether we had planned on a meeting of that length was immaterial. As I believe I mentioned earlier, these people meant business. They understood exactly the type of offenders that were housed in that clean, fresh-smelling facility, and no security measure would be ignored or considered overkill.

The deputy warden and every staff member we encountered that day were pleasant and businesslike. Their shoes and badges were as polished as the glass doors at the entrance. Their posture was square and alert, and their conversation was limited to the business at hand, nothing more and nothing less. Not one of them expressed the desire to be present when we met with Franklin; our purpose there was of no consequence to these people. Their concern was to make certain that every prisoner was accounted for at the end of the day. Not one of them gave me the impression that he would hesitate, even for a second, to shoot to kill should the need arise. We understood each other quite well.

Warden Miller had granted us the opportunity to meet with Franklin, but he had also made it very clear that he was a "special case," and "special arrangements" had to be made for the meeting. The deputy warden, satisfied that we understood the procedures, handed us off to an equally polite supervisor from the special holding area in which Franklin was housed. He took us deeper into Marion, past a spit-shined all-aluminum kitchen and down two flights of stairs. At the bottom of those stairs was a heavy-duty steel bar door, the entrance to the special holding unit for very high-risk inmates. Once again, our identities were established and verified, and then we were admitted. Sitting at a desk in the lobby area of this sub-basement-level cell block was a single guard. Behind him were rows of individual cells fronted by the same heavy-duty steel bars. Three feet behind those steel bars were the steel doors to the cells themselves. This deep into the belly of the beast, with the steel bar door locked behind us and rows of steel bars in front of us, I couldn't shake the disquieting feeling that the rest of the world was a world away, maybe even in another universe that ran parallel to this squeaky-clean, deathly quiet one in which my partner and I now found ourselves.

The guard on duty ushered us into a concrete cell directly across the lobby area from Franklin's. Once we were safely in the cell, Franklin was brought in, and the three of us were locked in that cell together for the duration of the visit. I can close my eyes even now and remember the sound of that door closing behind the guard. It was a lonely, final sound. There was a small covered window in the door that could be opened by a guard anytime he wanted to check on us, and I had no doubt that there were closed circuit cameras both inside and outside the cell. I have never felt so isolated, though, as I did that day in that small concrete cell with Mac and Joseph Franklin.

The inmate's wrists and ankles were shackled, and not with those tiny chains that looked like something you might buy your wife for Christmas. The chains that wrapped around his wrists, torso, and ankles were heavyweight, more like anchor chains than jewelry.

One look at the man who stood before us was truly worth a thousand words. What I saw carved into his face in the lines and creases, but mostly what I saw behind those cold eyes (both calculating and desperate, if you can imagine that) that clearly regarded us as the enemy, told me an awful lot about Joseph Paul Franklin. From the look on Mac's face, he was getting the same read, and he did not like it one bit.

"Nice to meet ya. Call me Joe," he grinned, and extended his right hand as best he could, considering his awkward metal attire.

CHAPTER 7
The Disappearing Boy, the Emerging Man
(mid-1960s–1970s)

"PRAISE THE LORD," the pretty young girl said in unison with a mesmerized Jimmy Vaughn. She reached across the Formica-topped table and slipped her small hand into his. The couple was sitting at a back table in a Mobile diner and had just finished reading from the book of Ecclesiastes; she had reached a giddy delight as they did so. He on the other hand, looked studious, as if he had been left hanging, hungry for more. Her flirtatious reach across the table only distracted him for a moment; he glanced up from the text, then looked down again just as quickly, fidgeting with his glasses in a self-conscious attempt to divert her gaze from his injured eye. She didn't mind his appearance at all; some laughingly called him "lazy eye" or "four-eyes," but she thought Jimmy Vaughn was the most handsome boy she had ever seen. He was practically a man, in fact, and he was so smart. She was sure that, given enough time, she could win him over for Christ. She was also sure that, with a little bit more time and a lot more sex, she would win him over to marriage.

A wedding was the last thing that came to Jimmy's mind on these afternoons when they'd get together to read the Bible and usually, to fuck afterwards. There would be time for that and more later, if he played his cards right. Right now, he was pondering the God of the Old Testament. He liked Him. He didn't take any crap.

Jimmy had met the girl just a few weeks earlier. She was only fifteen, but that was all right with him. In fact, he preferred them younger. The ones his age talked too much. The young ones were easier to be with. They were thrilled just to be with someone older, and he was nineteen, almost twenty. And this one liked to have sex. Anytime he wanted it, she didn't seem to mind. Hell, she even liked it, or at least she did a good job of pretending that she did. Same thing, really. Girls like that didn't come along very often. Most of them wanted to play games, to tease him and then withhold the promise in exchange for whatever it was they wanted from him. Usually, what they wanted was marriage. He had already been that route, and the union hadn't lasted. Bobbie Louise Dorman was the girl's name. They met when she was sixteen years old, and two weeks later they married. Four months after that, they divorced. Things just hadn't worked out.

Jimmy couldn't see what the big deal was about marriage; there were bigger things going on in a bigger world that was spinning out of control, thanks to the niggers, Jews, and nigger and Jew lovers. He supposed most people didn't want to see what was happening in this country, because seeing it meant acknowledging it, and acknowledging it meant having to do something about it. Well he saw it, all right. And he was beginning to think that he was the only one who was willing to do something about it.

She continued to stare at him while she rubbed his palm with her soft, small fingers, tracing little lines to his wrist and back again. Her fluttery, suggestive meanderings began to distract him, and before long he was reacting in a very physical way to her unspoken invitation. His thoughts turned from God to her soft lips and thighs, and all of a sudden, the bigger problems of the bigger world didn't seem to matter so much. Almost every time they met like this, to go to church or to talk about the Bible or about God, they'd end up screwing. Hell, after church two

Sundays ago, they had sex in the woods right behind the building after the service. He considered himself to be pretty experienced when it came to sex, but he had never been as turned on as he was that Sunday afternoon in the mottled shade of the thin canopy of leaves behind the small Baptist church. He was pretty sure that some of the old high and mighty bitches that regularly sat on the front row got a glimpse of the young pair as they jerked and fumbled and grunted in the leaves and dirt just beyond the crudely carved cross at the edge of the gravel parking lot, but he didn't care. Neither did she, for that matter. That's what made it so exciting. This fifteen-year-old Bible-toting nymphomaniac wasn't the reason he had become so interested in going to church lately, but she sure didn't hurt matters none.

Church and religion fascinated Jimmy, so much so that he was in the process of visiting every single church he could find in the Mobile phone book. In the late 1960s, that was a whole lot of churches. Every one he visited had been a bit different from the last, but they all offered pretty much the same message. Salvation could be yours, said the preachers, pastors, and priests, if you would just admit to being a sinner and accept that Jesus Christ was who He said He was. He claimed to be the Son of God, but He also claimed to be the same as God (that was a hard pill for Jimmy to swallow, although everybody else seemed to understand it just fine). He wanted to believe the teachings of the Bible. He wanted to belong to the group of people who called themselves Christians. Still, he preferred the Old Testament God who was, ironically, the God of the Jews. He was a vengeful, jealous God, and His followers obeyed His laws strictly out of duty and fear. Jimmy liked that a lot.

The way Jimmy understood things, Jesus Christ could kill a man with a bolt of lightning if He chose to, but he never had and never would. He could summon thousands of angels to smite those who angered Him, but in all of His thirty-three years on earth, He never had. Jesus Christ's message was about love, forgiveness, and mercy. Jimmy was having a hard time digesting that message; it was much easier for him to understand the God of fear and punishment and misery. That God was more in line with a father, as Jimmy understood the term. He had heard an awful lot about a harsh, unforgiving God, spewed like red-orange lava from pulpits in Mobile and along the coast of Alabama. He had visited more than a dozen Southern Baptist churches alone, and the taste they'd left in his mouth was bitter, like a necessary medicine. He had also visited churches of God, churches of Christ, and Methodist churches; hell, he'd even crossed the threshold of a Catholic church, so desperate was he to find some answers and a sense of purpose. The concept of a Higher Being, of an entity that was all-knowing, one that exacted swift and stern punishment for even the slightest of transgressions, intrigued him. Whether his fascination was with God's vengeance or with Christians, he couldn't be sure. Not yet, anyway. He just knew that he longed to know more.

For all of his life, more than eighteen miserable years of it, he had never belonged to anything, not even to his own family. His parents were divorced, but that didn't matter to him. For as long as he could remember, his father had been gone, anyway. When he did show up (after months or sometimes years) on Helen Vaughn's front porch on the wrong side of the tracks in Mobile, he was drunk and mean. Helen, his mother, was just mean. He hated them both. He could hate them separately just as well as he could if they lived under the same roof, so divorce had nothing to do with the way he felt about them.

He didn't see his brother and sisters all that often. His brother Gordon spent a lot of time in and out of mental institutions and prison; by mere chance, he was spotted in 2015 on a Mobile, Alabama, newscast as a reporter interviewed homeless people in the city. Gordon, apparently, didn't fare very well as a result of his upbringing, either. His sisters were not spared the fallout of growing up in abuse and poverty, either. He supposed that seeing each other just brought all the terrible memories back, and who needed that?

He had never had friends; as a child, his mother insisted that he and his siblings remain isolated, save for the torturous hours he spent at school. When they would get home from school in the afternoons, she insisted that they sit on the couch and watch television until bedtime. Jimmy and Gordon would sneak out their bedroom window just so they could play with other neighborhood kids, but she would always catch them, and a beating always ensued. After a while, the boys just gave up. Because of that isolation and the relentless abuse doled out by his parents (and Jimmy had always taken the brunt of their anger), he trailed other young people his age, both physically and emotionally. While for years he had also trailed them intellectually, he was catching up at a steady pace. His intelligence was above average; the imbeciles with whom he went to school, and the ones who taught the classes, had begun to bore him. At age seventeen, he dropped out of Murphy High School altogether. He was a discipline problem and a poor student, and teachers and administrators were happy to see him go. His parents couldn't have cared less what he did with his time, and nobody else even noticed that he was gone.

While he wanted very much for Christianity (and the warmly accommodating fifteen-year-old) to fill the void in his life, it seemed that the black maw continued to grow no matter how much he fed it with scripture and sex.

Marriage had not satisfied the hunger in him; in fact, it had magnified it. He was still ravenous for a sense of belonging, but there was something more. Years later, he would understand that something to be pure hate, but as a young man it just felt like restlessness. He thought that this new girl might satisfy that hunger, with her open legs and her open Bible. She certainly fulfilled his physical needs. His appetite was fierce, for both the girl and the religion, but if he had had the proper words to put to it back then, he would have simply understood that he had a fierce need to rebel, and incite others to rebel, against an ever-growing, dark-skinned tyranny.

Something else had appeared on the horizon in recent months, a brewing thundercloud that had gotten Jimmy's attention and held onto it. The American Nazi Party had emerged from the red clay of Alabama and other dissatisfied southern states, and it was growing tall and strong, fertilized and tended by the whites' resentment of the government, and of course Jews, "niggers," and other inferior groups. The government was pandering to these populations in a way that made Jimmy physically and mentally sick. Why in his own neighborhood, the one in which he was raised, "niggers" were being handed money to pay rent and hell, to buy those houses. They were being given money to buy food, too, and God knows what else they were being handed. All because they were black. You think a white person could get that kind of help? Hell no, and it made him furious.

As it turned out, there were others—lots of them—who felt the same way. Racial hatred and division, while it had simmered for decades here in Mobile, was now at a full boil. People had had enough of having those they deemed inferior shoved down their throats. To Jimmy's way of thinking, at first anyway, the Nazis had the right idea. *Heil fucking Hitler.* He was hungry to know more about white supremacists, so he set about learning more about the American Nazi Party the same way he taught himself about Christianity: via research. To his dismay, he didn't think that even the Nazis were going to actually do something about the injustices. So far, all he heard was talk. Talk wasn't enough.

Jimmy's mind had wandered as he waited for the political meeting to commence. Memories of Bobbie Louise, of his childhood that stubbornly haunted him, and of the sweet fifteen-year-old and her wet religion had crept into his mind as the initial proceedings of the meeting droned on. The room, a gymnasium really, was filling with people, most of them men. There was one woman sitting at the table up front next to the podium, but she was here in an official capacity. *Must be here to take notes or something.* This official meeting of the American Nazi Party was about to come to order.

Yes, it had taken a while, but he had eventually visited every single church in Mobile, a feat that his sisters had found both amazing and intriguing, especially for such a young man. For a brief time in his late teens, he had even become a member of Garner Ted Armstrong's Church of God. But before long, he felt that familiar unrest and dissatisfaction. His insides always felt like there was a tiger pacing in there, pacing and watching for the chance to break free and kill its captors and tormentors. He knew that when he began to feel that way, it was time to make a change. It was time to try again to find people who thought like he did, people who were fed up enough to do something about the reverse discrimination and oppression that plagued the South.

By the time Jimmy reached twenty years of age, he was better able to identify both the tiger inside him, and the relentless pacing. There were wrongs in the world that had to be put right. There were blatant injustices. There were abominations. Blacks had become the focus of most of his hatred and unrest. Jews and other minorities had become the target of the rest of it. By 1970 or so, black families had infiltrated the federally assisted neighborhood in Mobile that Jimmy called home, and the same thing was happening across the south in cities of all sizes. The government was shoving them down good white people's throats like bad medicine, and it made him sick with fury. The feds—the damned White House, especially—were giving them handouts right and left, while they ground their boot heels into the necks of poor working white men to pay the tab. The morality of the American people had gone straight to hell, but nobody was doing anything about it. The churches weren't; all their preaching and wheedling and talk about eternal life and loving thy neighbor was just so much ineffective bullshit. They were teaching Christians that God loves everybody, no matter what color their skin was, and no matter what they might have done in life. They were preaching, for God's sake, acceptance and forgiveness. *You don't have to be a genius to know that blasphemy like that pisses God off.* By age twenty,

Jimmy had settled in his mind that the one true God was the God of the Old Testament, the one who kept tabs on the human race, kept track of every single transgression in a large, dusty ledger, the one who held grudges and exacted punishment in the most frightening and dreadful ways imaginable. No other God made sense to him.

The government sure as hell wasn't going to fix the problem of the niggers overtaking the cities and the Jews overtaking everything else. Hell, they were the problem. *Those assholes in Washington aren't going to do anything. They're the ones making things worse. When a government starts making white kids get on the same school buses as nigger kids, when it makes white kids sit in the same classrooms as nigger kids, it's gotten out of control. It's overstepped its boundaries. Somebody has got to stop this. It's immoral. It's wrong.* The Old Testament God would hate the mess that this country had become. He knew that much, anyway. And another thought had begun surfacing again and again in Jimmy Vaughn's mind: *God needs a soldier down here on earth. He needs boots on the ground to clean up this mess.*

These sentiments, this fringe mentality, had begun to mold and form Jimmy Vaughn, the man. In fact if a man passing him on the street had the ability to read Vaughn's twisted, burning mind, he would piss himself in terror. Thoughts of hatred and revenge had become the reason he got out of bed in the morning. They were the reason he fortified his body with clean food, and refused to drink alcohol or smoke cigarettes. They were the reason he exercised. They were the reason he had migrated from the mainstream Christian church to more rigid beliefs, the reason he had gotten very familiar and comfortable with all types of firearms, even learning how to shoot left-handed in order to accommodate his bad eye. James Clayton Vaughn was preparing. There was a war coming, and he was looking for like-minded white Americans with whom to ally himself. He was looking for other white supremacists to join with him in a war against those he deemed inferior and the government who forced them on hard-working white Americans. The outcome was predetermined, of that he was sure. There could be no outcome but a white victory, a righting of the wrongs that had come to define the sorry state of the country. God was on his side.

That was why he sat here, in this hard plastic chair, as this meeting of the American Nazi Party was called to order. He had lately become affiliated with a church that taught British Israelism, its doctrine teaching that western Europeans are the real direct descendants of the ten lost tribes of Israel. In other words, those who claimed to be Jews had in fact usurped that distinction from the actual Jews, the rightful ones. He believed in white supremacy and racial purity, and he hated both Jews (the impostor Jews, anyway) and blacks.

A young man, about twenty-five years old, stood in uniform on the stage in the front of the room, behind a podium and in front of a large red and black swastika. His head was clean-shaven, and his eyes were blue, bright and sharp. He began to address the crowd of about a hundred fifty or so white men, who ranged in age from their late teens to their late fifties. The men were mostly lower income, blue collar, beaten down, and fed up.

The sharp blue-eyed man cleared his throat, then leaned toward the microphone. "We demand that, in order to become a citizen of the state, one must first be a deserving Aryan," the young man stated as the microphone whined and buzzed with his initial words. The men in the room cheered and rose to their feet. Jimmy leaned in, as though he was listening intently, but his mind wandered back to the diner in Mobile. He let it. He had heard all this before. While he loved the American Nazi party it was becoming frustratingly clear that, at least this particular arm of it, was all talk and no action. After several months, they were already losing his interest. The tiger was pacing; it was time for a change.

He let his mind wander back to the diner. Jimmy paid the tab not long after their Bible reading had ended, left a meager tip, and the two of them walked out into the suffocating heat of a late afternoon that only Mobile, Alabama, can serve up, stifling and steamy. They walked hand in hand along the sidewalk, looking into storefronts and not saying a word. The girl was in love, or as close to love as a girl that age can get. Jimmy, however, was agitated, frustrated. He liked her just fine, but aside from her eager willingness to have sex with him and read the Bible, he found her boring. As she gazed up at him with hopeful adoration, he was already silently searching for a reason to part company with her for the afternoon. He was restless. Maybe it was the heat, but he didn't think so. Though he was a young man, he knew enough about himself to know that agitation and frustration could quickly mushroom into violence. He knew it, Bobbie Louise knew it, and any girl that had ever been with him for very long knew it. He had always felt sorry afterward for the beatings he had given them, but he never seemed to be able to stop himself.

As he and the young girl walked along in that buzzing silence that only young lovers can manufacture (she dreaming of a house and a white picket fence, he devising a plan to get rid of her for the afternoon), Jimmy stopped short, squeezing the girl's hand as he did. "You gotta be fucking kidding me. No way in hell." Without saying a word to his young companion, he sprinted across the street, dodging a few cars, horns honking and brakes shrieking as he went. He was headed straight for the other side of the street, straight for another young couple walking hand in hand. The woman was white and the man, black. Jimmy's head pounded; he never took his eyes off the mixed couple as he ran toward them. Safely across the street through no fault of his own, Jimmy stopped short, standing directly in their path. They hadn't noticed him yet, but any second now, they would. He'd make damn sure of that. The fury in his head was whirring out of control; he could hear his companion's whining voice from somewhere in the distance, sounding as though she were in another world and not just on the other side of the street. If she had been within his reach, he would have throttled her right there on the street in broad daylight. Her damned voice sounded like a screeching screen door.

"Jimmy! What are you doing? Where are you going?" The burning red edges of his vision that would eventually turn gray, so familiar to him by now, were creeping in. Soon, he would struggle to maintain control of his actions.

The woman saw him first. She stopped, eyes wide in disbelief as she tried to register exactly what she was seeing, and opened her mouth to say something to her companion. Jimmy advanced, then stopped short, within inches of the couple. Looking directly at the woman, he hissed, "That's disgusting, and you're a whore." His spittle landed on her eyelashes, some of it even in her mouth, which was hanging open in both shock and fear. She could smell the sweat on him. She could smell his sour breath. Sounds were coming out of her mouth, but they were unintelligible. It was always the same.

The couple just stood there, not knowing what to say, not knowing whether their assailant was armed or perhaps insane. Even in the late 1960s in Mobile, such an open confrontation was rare unless there were mobs involved, angry crowds being led by agitators sprinkled among them. Racism usually reared its ugly head, in public anyway, in packs, not one on one, face to face like this. The man moved in front of the woman as he pushed her behind him, putting himself between Jimmy and her. The move was instinctual, protective. What they were witnessing with their own eyes was not making sense to either of them.

"You're both gonna burn in hell," Jimmy muttered as he blocked their way, not letting them pass. As soon as he'd said his piece and spat rudely on the concrete at their feet, Jimmy turned and looking both ways, crossed the four lanes of traffic that separated him from the shocked girl waiting on the other side. He joined hands with her again, squeezing hers a little too tight for comfort. He was quiet, but she could see that he was seething. He was dragging her along behind him, not ambling sweetly as he had been doing before his outburst.

"Jimmy . . . ?" she began, and he cut her off before she could ask what was wrong.

"Shut the fuck up," he snapped. "I'm getting sick and tired of seeing them everywhere I go. They've taken over the neighborhood and hell, the whole damned city. They walk around in public like that like they have a right. Well they don't, and every time I see a white woman with a nigger, I'm going to tell them that they don't."

The young girl walked the rest of the way home with her lover in silence. Even she had lost her appetite for sex this afternoon. All she wanted to do was get home, go up to her room, and maybe take a nap. Anything to erase the embarrassing display she had just witnessed. She wanted to explain to Jimmy that Jesus wouldn't have done what he did today, that Christ loved everyone the same, but she didn't dare. She had never seen him like this, and she felt that she had just stumbled upon one of many lines that were not to be crossed in what turned out to be their very brief but turbulent relationship.

Where did the hate come from? Jimmy himself couldn't answer that question, at least not back then. He wouldn't have been able to put words to the answer. Federal open housing legislation had rolled out the red carpet for families of all races (and in the 1960s, that meant black families) in the Vaughns' neighborhood. *They had just waltzed right on in like they had a right.* The federal government had mandated the integration of schools, and that had just thrown gasoline on the blazing fire of hate and resentment among many whites. *Who the hell were those fat cats in Washington to pass such a law, with all of their precious children enrolled in their snotty, lily-white private schools up north?* As was typical anytime rampant and jarring integration took place in the Deep South during those fitful years of the '60s and '70s, segregationist groups awoke, stretched, and flexed their mean muscles. Pockets of violence broke out almost weekly, and every now and then, peaceful marches would erupt in divided aggression, then escalate to looting and violence. The cycle, nothing new to a southerner, was simply a way of life; it was as old as the very soil here.

One spring day in 1967, just before Jimmy dropped out of Murphy High School, a classmate handed him a leaflet printed and circulated by the Ku Klux Klan. Jimmy read it once, then twice; he carried it with him wherever he went. Soon after reading that first missive laced with hate and division, he attended his first Klan meeting. He was not looking for friends; he was looking for fellow soldiers. He didn't know it at the time, but he was also looking for belonging, something he had never known. The clandestine group and the message they carried came closer to calming that pacing tiger in his gut than Christianity could ever hope to. He soaked up their racist rantings and white superiority jargon like a dry sponge squeezed tight and submerged in cool, purifying water. Yes, the Klan was intriguing, and it had held his interest off and on for a while now, but there was still something missing, and that was action. Meaningful action. All the talk in the world about the sorry state of affairs in this country didn't do a damned thing to change it. Klansmen could hold a meeting every week in every city in the South, but nothing was going to change until somebody took the lead and did whatever was necessary to be the flint that ignited a cleansing, fire-and-brimstone war between the races. A very necessary war, according to Jimmy, which would set things right, one that would put niggers and Jews and every other inferior race in their proper place—far beneath the pure white race, the race that God loved above all others. Every day, Jimmy Vaughn believed a little more, then a little more, that he was the soldier to start that war. Nothing in his life mattered to him more than the hate that he had begun to wear like a badge of honor. He could sense that bigger things were coming, that he alone was the man who had the courage and the talents to set things straight in this godforsaken mess of a country. He alone knew that the sickening pandering and race mixing would not come to an end until the streets ran with blood. Not just any blood, mind you. Jew blood. Nigger blood.

The blood of the mealy-mouthed politicians who were lining their pockets with the hard-earned money of white men. Yes, bigger things were coming. He could feel it.

Women did not fill his need for belonging; in fact, mostly all they did was frustrate and infuriate him. They were good for one thing and one thing only, and while that one thing was fleetingly pleasant, it could not cool the hate. Christianity was nice, he supposed, but it didn't have anything to do with real life. And Jesus Christ? He made no sense at all to Jimmy Vaughn. No matter what the Bible or history or any newfangled preacher behind the pulpit had to say, Jimmy knew for a fact that Jesus Christ was a white man. He had to be. He seemed to be pretty smart, from what Jimmy had read, even if He was a bit misguided. But He was white, that much was obvious, in his mind. Nothing else made sense. But why would a white man (a man who claimed to be God, no less) have all that power at His fingertips to kill and maim and smite, and never use it? What was the purpose of that? Christianity was a nice idea, he supposed, for someone who had the luxury of turning the other cheek, but it wasn't for him.

The Klan had the right idea; whites are superior and as such, the race should be kept pure and protected. But what the hell was the Klan doing about it? Crying and marching, that was about it. He remembered a news story he had seen a couple of months ago. The reporter was standing in the foreground, and behind her were two hundred or so Ku Klux Klansmen, marching in a small city in Georgia. "Peacefully demonstrating," the reporter said, as the cameraman panned the crowd of demonstrators. Jimmy thought the whole thing was stupid. "They look like a bunch of whipped dogs," he sneered as he watched the TV that was bolted to the floor in his cheap motel room. He seethed with rage, hating what white men had been reduced to. And while the news reporter droned on and on about the indignance of area residents and the outdated mantra of the Klan, the cops showed up and told the crowd to disperse. To Jimmy's disgust, that's exactly what they did. *Pussies turned tail and ran when they were told to.* He was filled with disgust and loathing when he saw that. In fact, it might have been that very day that James Clayton Vaughn accepted his purpose in life. For all their noisemaking, marching, and peaceful bullshit demonstrating, the Klan was about as effective as a giggling klatch of high school cheerleaders. Besides, he was convinced that the organization was lousy with FBI informants. He had read somewhere that in one southern chapter of forty-one Klansmen, forty of those were informants. *No wonder they can't get anything done, stupid assholes.* And so his search continued for a group with which he could align himself, a group from which other God-fearing white men would walk alongside him, a group with a clear vision and enough courage to clean house, as his mother used to say in her infinite wisdom.

It was his discovery of one particular book that changed Jimmy's life forever. No one had loaned it to him or given it to him, or even recommended it to him. He saw it on the shelf, and having overheard other kids in school talk about it, he stole it from the library in high school in 1965, when he was just fifteen years old. The book was a copy of *Mein Kampf,* and reading it awakened something in his soul that he never dreamed existed. It awakened purpose. Hitler's writings answered questions for Jimmy that Jesus Christ could not, no matter how hard Jimmy tried to believe He could. Hitler's words were divinely inspired (by a white, Old Testament God, no doubt), and they spoke directly to him, right into his soul. They moved him to action. He read the book cover to cover several times during the years that followed. As he shared with CNN reporter Kyung Lah from death row in Missouri, awaiting execution in 2013, "I had this real strange feeling in my mind," when he read Adolf Hitler's manifesto. "I've never felt that way about any other book that I read. It was something weird about that book." Finally, Jimmy Vaughn had found something he could belong to, people who shared common beliefs with him. For the first time in his miserable life, he felt as though he was part of a family. He was home.

Before she packed up and left him, Bobbie Louise said in a *People Magazine* interview, she would often come upon her husband practicing Nazi salutes in the mirror. Other days, she would walk in on him to find him sobbing uncontrollably. Not long after those episodes began, she found crudely stitched swastikas on several of his shirts. His eating habits changed; he began to follow food fads and trends almost as religiously as he followed the teachings of Hitler.

For a short time, he even gravitated toward the teachings and example of Charles Manson. Manson was a man of vision and drive. He too called for a war between the races, one that would inevitably drive the black man back down to his place in society, while it lifted up the white man to his place of superiority.

Jimmy had his idols and examples. He had his vision. He had burning hate, a powerful motivator. During his late teens and early twenties, he steeped himself in the teachings of both the Nazi party and the Ku Klux Klan. He began to drift, traveling to the northeast United States, then back down south, then a little to the west, then south again. His ability and willingness to move about the country freely and unfettered was the beginning of the misty formation of Jimmy Vaughn's ghost-like character. He had no friends, he had no ties. He had no loyalties to anyone or any group except whites. By the early 1970s, he had become little more to law enforcement than a mere nuisance, a petty criminal who had racked up a few low-level weapons charges, driving violations, and such. But his vision and determination were clear and growing. He joined the National States Rights Party in 1973, hoping that their rigid opposition to the federal government's mandates (such as integration in schools) might compel visionaries to take up arms. They talked a good game, but Jimmy could not find even one other soldier to join him in his crusade to start a war between the races. Not one. Not giving up on what he believed to be a divine quest, he joined the KKK in Atlanta in 1976.

That same year, he sent a threatening letter to newly elected president Jimmy Carter, warning him not to pander to inferiors, not to push what he called the "nigger agenda." If he did, there would be consequences. That one letter placed him on the outer edge of the FBI's curious radar, as no one—not even the most clever agent—could have possibly imagined the true threat that festered inside James Clayton Vaughn. Any threat to a US president got the FBI's attention, but still, no one knew enough about the author of that letter to consider him more than a fringe crackpot. Not yet, they didn't.

A turning point came in 1976, when he legally changed his name from James Clayton Vaughn to Joseph Paul Franklin, in honor of Benjamin Franklin (a rebel and a visionary in his own right) and his beloved idol, Joseph Goebbels. On Labor Day of that same year in Atlanta, he spotted and followed an interracial couple in a park, loudly berating them and ultimately, spraying them with mace. This was his first known physical attack on another person, but it certainly would not be his last. The boy had finally become a man, and he would not be dissuaded from what he now knew to be his purpose.

CHAPTER 8
A Friend in Need
(early 1980s)

Detective Michael Cowart

Aside from *Mein Kampf*, the closest thing Joe Franklin ever had to a friend was a young man named Joe Kitts. It is my opinion, as well as the opinion of the other detectives with whom I worked on this case, that Franklin befriended Kitts strictly as a matter of convenience.

Joe Kitts was a little bit younger than Franklin, and very easily led. The two men met when Franklin lived in Atlanta, as he did off and on over the years. Kitts and his mother, a bent, haggard-looking woman, lived in an apartment off Hairston Road in DeKalb County. The woman had lived a hard, worry-filled life, and it showed on her face and in her posture. She hated cops. I suppose I couldn't really blame her. Her son was in hot water with law enforcement quite often, and she had gotten so used to covering for him and answering for him that the stress was deeply etched into her drawn and tired face. If I had to guess her age simply by looking at her, I'd say that she was in her late sixties. I think she was actually in her early forties at the time we first met and talked with her son.

Whether Joe Kitts was born with a mental deficiency, or his brain had simmered in drugs and alcohol for too long, who knows?

But he served a couple of purposes for Joe Franklin, and that's all that mattered. Franklin needed a flunkie, a gofer, a tool really, someone eager to please and easily deceived, and Kitts fit the bill on all counts. Franklin could get him to run errands or whatever needed to be done, and Kitts never asked questions. He was in awe of Joe Franklin and would do whatever he asked, without ever asking anything in return. The whole notion of Joe Franklin blazing the trail for a race war fascinated Kitts. When he was in Joe's presence, he felt as though he was in the company of a real celebrity. But there was another reason that Franklin needed Kitts, a more important reason, and that was his own frail but ravenous ego.

In the years during which Franklin lived as a drifter, he would often stay at the apartment of Joe Kitts and his mother. While Mrs. Kitts did not particularly care for Franklin, she allowed him those brief stays just the same. Her son had a lack of friends or even acquaintances; the ones he did have were either selling drugs or looking to use them with her son. While she didn't like Joe Franklin much at all, what with his unannounced visits and the firearms he always seemed to carelessly show off in her home, at least she could rest assured that he did not use drugs or bring them into her home. Whatever else he was, he was not a user or an alcoholic. That was his only redeeming quality, but for Joseph Kitts's mother, it was enough. She would feed Franklin and sometimes even lend him a bit of money here and there. There were several theories among investigators as to why she allowed Joe Franklin the liberty of occasionally living in her home, but I believe I know exactly why she did it. She loved her son, and she would do whatever she could to make him happy.

When Joe Franklin would pop in unannounced for one of his brief stays, he and Kitts and his mother would dine on whatever meager meal she had prepared that evening, and afterward, she would excuse herself to her bedroom while the two men talked. With an audience of just one mesmerized, gullible listener, Joe Franklin shone. Telling his tales to Kitts, he actually became the man he longed to be. He became a soldier for The Cause, the white man's hero and the black man's darkest fear. Joe Franklin, on those evenings, would regale Kitts with exciting stories of his latest adventures: bank robberies, burglaries, shootings, weapons thefts, and disposals. Every now and then, he would even throw in a tall tale or two about his latest female conquests (Franklin fancied himself a real ladies man; the younger the lady, the better as far as he was concerned). Yes, in Kitts's eyes, Joe Franklin was what he needed to be: a larger-than-life warrior, a champion for the white race.

On one occasion, after finishing a fine meal of beef stew with the Kitts family, Franklin told the younger man about a recent burglary he had committed in Athens, Georgia, legendary home of the University of Georgia. He said, with some pride, that he had broken into a gun shop and stolen thousands of dollars worth of firearms. Kitts, all five-foot-seven, drunk, disheveled inches of him, listened to Franklin's story mesmerized, unblinking. He took another long, sloppy gulp from the bottle of cheap vodka Joe had brought him, wiped his mouth with the back of his hand, and settled back into the sofa as Joe continued telling him about the daringly dangerous heist and the cache of weapons he now had in his possession as a result of it.

"Well what the hell did you do with all them guns?" Kitts asked in his customary drunken slur. Even in his foggy state, he knew that Joe Franklin had no place to keep such a large stash of weapons. He didn't even have a permanent address.

"I buried them, under that bridge down near Grady," he answered, a sly smile spreading across his face. He was referring to Grady Hospital, in the heart of downtown Atlanta. Not far from Fulton County Stadium, where the Atlanta Braves played baseball and the Atlanta Falcons played football, Grady was and still is a behemoth of a hospital surrounded by an eclectic mix of poverty, crime, and education, with Georgia State University just a few blocks away.

Dan, Mac, and I did our best to dig up whatever informa-tion we could on any burglaries in or near Athens and Clarke County during the timeframe to which Franklin referred. We did find police reports about a gun shop burglary in which several pistols were stolen. Based on that discovery, we then dug up the dry, stubborn earth under the only bridge near Grady Hospital at the time, looking for the haul of weapons Franklin said he had buried there. Nothing. I remain convinced to this day that Franklin concocted that story for the sole reason of telling it to Joe Kitts, his one true admirer. What better way to pay homage to his idol, Joseph Goebbels, who was known for strategically burying weapons and cash? The Propaganda Minister of Nazi Germany was a wartime genius.

Of course, Franklin was not above using his devoted admirer whenever he saw fit. I recall, for instance, that Franklin told us during an interview at the Marion prison that he regularly used Kitts's name, address, and social security number to obtain false IDs. We found proof of that in Alabama. I believe he had that same false ID on him when he was questioned for shooting the manager of a Taco Bell restaurant in Doraville, Georgia.

Curiously, when I talked with Joe Franklin in both the Marion and the Chattanooga prisons, he discussed openly and freely his involvement with bombings, shootings, and bank robberies, easily providing details about any of them. When I'd touch on the story about burglarizing the gun shop and burying the haul, however, he would fidget, stammer, and refuse to make eye contact with me, even for a second. I believe that he did that because he was lying about the whole thing, from start to finish. I was getting to know him very well, or at least as well as anyone ever really knew him. That bothered me. It bothered me to think that I knew Joseph Paul Franklin at all, much less as well as I did. Being in his pres-ence was unsettling, very disturbing. He was perhaps the most dangerous man I had ever encountered, and I truly believe that with time, he actually considered me to be his friend.

In the end, once Franklin had been incarcerated and sentenced to several life terms for various murders, Kitts must have felt very sure that he would never get out of prison and see the light of day again. That was lucky for us indeed, because when we were investigating the possibility of Franklin having shot Larry Flynt and Gene Reeves, Kitts was never very hard to find, and for fifty dollars or so, he'd tell Bruno and me anything we wanted to know about Franklin and his claims. He was also trying to wrangle himself out of aggravated assault charges over in Cobb County (a suburb of Atlanta), so he was usually very eager to share information with us when we asked him to.

Over the years, the dark-haired, rumpled, often drunk Kitts had become a mere shell of the younger man he had once been. His mother had long since died, and he lived alone. I suppose that drugs, alcohol, and the company we keep do have a lasting effect on us over the years. When all was said and done, not even Joe Kitts had turned out to be a loyal friend to Franklin.

If there ever was a loner, Joseph Paul Franklin was it.

CHAPTER 9

Peaches, Vengeance, and The Head of the Snake
(1978)

AT THE CENTER of the quaint county seat in Gwinnett was an old Romanesque courthouse, the treasure box that held all the county's secrets and shames, an historic government building that dated back to 1885. From his vantage point here on Perry Street, Franklin couldn't see the entire stately old building situated comfortably over there on Crogan Street, but he knew that was the main place of business that people—two or three here, six or eight there—were either leaving or approaching on this fine gift of a morning. Important-looking men wearing business suits and carrying briefcases walked with purpose along the straight, white sidewalks. Women in tight, knee-length skirts and silky blouses with bows tied at the neck made their way through town, too. From the looks of them, most of them worked at the courthouse, answering official phones or shuffling official papers, facilitating, documenting, and validating the legal fleecing and screwing of the regular, hardworking folks here in Gwinnett County and surrounding parts.

This town, like so many others in this region of the South, was teetering on the fence that divided the pastoral from the urban. Sprinkled in with the businesspeople he had seen were farmers in red clay-stained overalls, aproned shopkeepers, and a few construction workers wearing hardhats. All that suited him just fine, because he was an expert at blending into a crowd, at being invisible while he went about his business. He had learned from experience the more people, the better. The more diversity, the better.

At the very top of the old courthouse was a large clock with big, black Roman numerals on it. He couldn't see it from here, but if he closed his eyes and shut out everything else, he could hear it. Picture it. That clock kept the time for all the townspeople, all the businesses gathered at the edge of the courthouse's four-sided lawn (already turning green with the fleeting warmth of a few March days), and all of the people who had ventured into town to take care of some business. In just a little while, the clock would strike noon, and if he had done his homework as well as he thought he had, as well as he usually did, it would be time.

Gwinnett County was no different from most other small Southern counties in 1978. It had its share of secrets and tragedies, just the same as any other, some of them dating back more than a hundred years. This used to be Creek Indian territory, for one thing. Landowners in the area had owned and traded slaves before the Civil War, for another. But there were other things, too—scandalous sex that had been swept under the rug with a few thousand dollars, political mischief, land stealing, child selling, you name it. And then there were the bizarre things, things that could and would only happen in a small, Southern, no-name town. Just ten years ago, in 1968, Emory University co-ed Barbara Jane Mackle was kidnapped and buried alive right here in this county, over in a heavily wooded area down near a city named Duluth (pronounced *DOO*-looth by Gwinnett old timers). For a ransom of $500,000 demanded of her father, Mackle's captors planned to purchase a yacht to widen the span of their illegal immigrant smuggling operation. As Franklin read about the kidnapping when he began to study the area, he was incensed. It didn't bother him that the woman had been kidnapped; that he could chalk up to her own stupidity. Rather, it bothered him to think that Mexicans and other lesser beings were being smuggled into the country. *Hard to imagine that shit. Bringing more inferiors here, like we don't have enough already.*

The FBI had swooped down upon the largely rural county then, and set up their command center in Lawrenceville. The case was solved, of course. The co-ed was found alive (if not quite well), and her captors were put on trial and sent to prison. Justice, in one form or another, had been served.

He had read somewhere that Barbara Jane Mackle later befriended her captors while they were still in prison. *Dumb bitch, just like all the rest. Served her right, then.*

Historically, this area had had more than its share of scandal and tragedy. If small towns have their secrets and shames (and rest assured that all of them do), then their county seats are where those secrets have been documented and filed away, and an old courthouse like the one in Lawrenceville is a memory box of sorts for the disputes, evils, and tragedies that settle in and take up residence through the years. Even though the first courthouse and all those old documents burned down to the ground back in 1871, a bigger, better building was erected in its place. There were plenty of official papers being signed, notarized, and pushed across desks every day in that courthouse. There were even more papers being carefully tucked away in gray metal file cabinets, in unmarked file folders, for the eyes of a few only. And every day, more of those file cabinets are loaded onto hand trucks and trundled carefully down to the damp, dark basement of the fancy courthouse building. They leave a carefully ordered paper trail that enables the rich to take from the poor, a whore of a wife to leave her hardworking husband, and a man with a briefcase to take everything from a man without one.

Small town secrets and shames. "Everything comes home to roost," his mother used to say, and even though he loathed the woman, he supposed that was true.

Even with all that to consider, Franklin wasn't interested in what was going on in the county courthouse today; it was what was going on in the state courthouse just up the street that interested him.

In 1977, Larry Flynt himself, the flamboyant publisher of *Hustler* Magazine, decided to come down to Atlanta to peddle his filthy publication out of a newsstand called Stan's Shopette down in Lilburn, Georgia. It was Flynt's way of thumbing his nose at the staunchly conservative laws governing obscenity and pornography in the Southern states. It was his way of waving his middle finger at the Jerry Falwells of the world, who did everything they could to stop the sale and distribution of *Hustler* and other similar publications in the South. For his efforts, both Fulton and Gwinnett counties in Georgia slapped him with obscenity charges; though only misdemeanors, the hullabaloo surrounding the entire matter was nothing short of a three-ring circus, with Flynt emerging as the proud ringmaster. The good old boys in Georgia in 1977 were by no means willing to accommodate the likes of *Hustler* or Larry Flynt.

The trial in Gwinnett County got under way in March 1978. The matter was being tried in the state courthouse, not too far from both the county courthouse and the old boarding house in which Franklin was now secretly ensconced.

The circus that seemed to follow Flynt wherever he went had settled in right here in Lawrenceville a few days before the trial began. Attorneys, expert witnesses, and even a celebrity or two had been parading in and out of the state court building ever since the trial commenced three days ago, and Franklin knew their comings and goings as well as his own. He had read in yesterday's paper that Wardell Pomeroy, one of the authors of the filthy Kinsey Reports on human sexuality, had come to town to back up Flynt's first amendment argument. A sex report. *Perverts, right here in Georgia of all places. Bet that cost you a pretty penny. Well the show's almost over, you sick sack of shit. Enjoy it while you can.*

Flynt and his paid entourage were staying over at the Holiday Inn on Pleasantdale Road during the trial. For himself, he had chosen to set up camp in the Golfland Motel, a little farther down I-85 and just across the Gwinnett County/DeKalb County line. He had registered under the name of James A. Cooper, one of his many aliases. He checked into Room 120 on March 4, and checked out on March 6. He did not return to that motel until November of that same year, when he went back to the same area to sell his Gran Torino. These details would come to light a few years from now, when Franklin's possible connection to the Larry Flynt shooting would be closely examined by law enforcement agents.

According to television and newspaper accounts concerning the progress of the trial, things were going very well for Flynt. As much as that irked him, Franklin didn't care about that one way or the other. He was there for the bigger picture, so to speak. Today, Flynt's luck would take a turn for the worse.

From what he had been able to learn simply by observing, Joe knew that court got started at about 8:00 every morning. At around 11:00 a.m., Larry Flynt and local criminal defense attorney Gene Reeves would exit the courthouse and walk the two blocks or so to the V&J Cafeteria for lunch, a favorite spot for area businessmen and attorneys. Both men would have a salad, because according to Reeves, they were trying to "watch their waistlines." In fact, in the last year or so, Reeves had already lost about one hundred pounds. In March of 1978, he was feeling better than he had in years.

About an hour or so after leaving the courthouse and eating lunch at the popular diner, the pair would walk back together the same way they came, and the afternoon court session would begin. *Today we're gonna change things up a little bit. Today I'm gonna teach you about respecting your own race, motherfucker.*

Gene Reeves was not one of Flynt's fancy New York lawyers. He was a Southern man, born in Meridian, Mississippi, and a well-respected criminal defense attorney with an office right on the square in the Gwinnett County seat. Having practiced law for fourteen years by 1978, Reeves was also forty-eight years old by then and had tried at least one hundred murder, rape, and other capital felony cases. He was as tenacious as a bulldog in the courtroom, a ferocious defender by all accounts. By his own admission, his measured Southern drawl often lured witnesses into the belief that he was somehow slow (a common mistake "outsiders" make with southerners), or that he was more interested in having a conversation than he was in tearing apart a testimony. By the time a cross examination was over, however, Reeves had made it very clear that he was neither slow nor interested in friendly conversation. From a very young age, Gene Reeves loved the law, and he believed with all his heart that no matter how despicable the charges against a man, that man deserved to be defended. Detective Michael Cowart himself had been called to testify in court on many occasions when Reeves was the defense attorney, and while the two men were on friendly terms outside the courthouse, Cowart said that Reeves was a formidable defender during a trial.

Also by Reeves's own admission, his demanding work schedule had put a terrible strain on his family life, and his devotion to his career had been hard on his wife and daughter. His profession had taken a toll on him as well; just two years earlier he had given up whiskey for good, and that in itself was a hard thing to do. His love of the law, paired with his unyielding belief that every man had the right to a fierce defense, had eaten away at him. Gene Reeves was privy to some appalling crimes and confidences, and sometimes numbing himself with drink was his only comfort. Whiskey and its whispered reassurances had helped him cope with his profession, but it had also quietly eroded his small family. It had been only recently that Reeves had begun to rebuild the things that had been broken for so long. Sometimes he wondered whether it was his job or his attempt to escape it that had derailed his life while he wasn't looking. Most times, he concluded that it really didn't matter. What mattered was fixing the problems he owned as best he could. In March 1978, he was doing just that. The invitation from Flynt's legal team to help choose a six-person jury for the obscenity trial had come along at a very good time. Not only did Reeves know the lay of the land and the way these bumpkins viewed what they called indecent, but Reeves would also come in handy by keeping Flynt occupied during the trial. Always inquisitive and stubbornly outspoken, Flynt could be a handful in a courtroom. With Reeves on board, Flynt's sharp attorneys could do their job while Reeves kept the pugnacious publisher entertained. Yes, things were finally starting to look up for Gene Reeves.

Reeves proved to be valuable in Flynt's defense. Who knew which direction the wind was blowing better than a lawyer from these parts? Reeves had earned himself a reputation in Gwinnett County for aggressively defending his clients but more important, he knew most everybody in the county. He knew exactly how folks here in the South felt about filth like *Hustler* magazine, and he could read people like books by asking them a few simple, but cleverly directed, questions.

Historically, Georgia has always made up a big chunk of the Bible Belt; back in the '60s and '70s, people didn't take kindly to pornography being displayed and sold in stores. It was an abomination. Reeves himself didn't much like what Flynt did for a living, but he'd fight to the death defending his right to do it. In fact, when Flynt asked Reeves what he thought about his tawdry magazine, Reeves answered, "I think it's filth, but I don't have to look at it, do I?" Flynt hired him on the spot, calling him the only honest attorney he'd ever met.

Gene Reeves couldn't remember a day when he didn't love the law with a burning passion. In his opinion, *Hustler* magazine was disgusting. But he was passionate about defending Flynt's right to publish it under the First Amendment's guarantee of free speech. Lawyers were funny that way. They would argue to the death a viewpoint that wasn't necessarily theirs. An ordinary man would call that dishonest or even crazy, but a lawyer just called it a job.

As it turned out, dying was very nearly what was required of Reeves in his brief service to the outspoken and opinionated porn king.

Unlike the self-righteous people of the state of Georgia, Joseph Franklin didn't really care that Larry Flynt produced and sold pornography for a living. He didn't spend his own money on it of course, but a lot of other men did. All he ever did was thumb through the nudie magazines at newsstands and convenience stores, but he never actually bought one of them. In Franklin's mind, buying the dirty magazines would be disgusting. But huddling in the far corner of a convenience store, perusing the filthy rag, was acceptable. Truth be told (and Franklin would never admit this until years later, when he met a detective whom he actually considered his friend), he admired Flynt's work. He enjoyed looking at women in all kinds of provocative positions. He especially loved the gynecologically graphic photos for which Flynt's magazine had become famous. The images in *Hustler* were not tastefully altered shots that whispered suggested sexuality. They were raw, up-close shots of a woman's sex, the pretty and the ugly of it. Yes, he admired the fact that Flynt didn't try to compete with *Playboy* and *Penthouse* by shoving "intellectual" or "responsible" articles in between the photos of randy couples fucking like animals. No, Flynt ran features like *Chester the Molester*, a regular feature about a fictitious child molester. Now that was entertainment. That was interesting.

It wasn't the fact that Flynt was a depraved pornographer that bothered Franklin. It was the shockingly filthy spread a couple of years ago in *Hustler* magazine titled "Butch—a Black Stud and His Georgia Peach," that made his blood boil when he first saw it. The groundbreaking feature in the December 1975 issue of *Hustler* presented a sickening display of sexually explicit photos of a black man with a white woman. They were doing all kinds of disgusting things, sexual things, things a mixed-race couple should never be allowed to do, much less be photographed doing. *He was fucking her, and the bitch looked for all the world like she was enjoying it. She was taking him into her mouth, and he was smiling! Laughing, maybe?* Maybe it wasn't just the presence of the pictures that had set him off, maybe it was the fact that the woman looked like she was having such a good time in them that pushed him over the edge.

Franklin would never forget the first time he saw that December 1975 issue of *Hustler*, predictably thumbing through the magazine at a busy Atlanta newsstand, with no intention of buying it. Slowly turning the pages, he took in every last detail of the photographs of the trashy women, some impossibly young and others, revoltingly old. They all wore too much makeup and if they were wearing clothes at all, the material was filmy and scant. Joe Franklin was thoroughly enjoying the Christmas issue of *Hustler*, ignoring the angry glances from the newsstand manager. "You gonna buy that thing or marry it?" the snotty man asked as Franklin leisurely thumbed through the magazine, just like he used to do with the new comic books at the neighborhood Quik-Mart. But Franklin barely heard the man's angry snipes, as he turned a page and got a first look at that month's shocking feature display. His blood turned cold as he looked at the things that black animal and the white whore were doing in the photographs. The degradation of white women made him sick. To Franklin, interracial couples were an abomination, an affront to God himself and not to be tolerated. The photos in the magazine nauseated him, turned his stomach, and a familiar rage began to build in him. The day that Franklin (who was still Jimmy Vaughn at the time) stood at that Atlanta newsstand and thumbed through the Christmas 1975 issue of *Hustler* was the day that Larry Flynt became a marked man.

CHAPTER 10
The Trial
(1978)

"IT IS NOT just freedom for the thought you love, but freedom for the thought you hate most," Larry Flynt explained to Gene Reeves. The two men sat at a small table in the back corner of the diner, discussing the breadth and depth of the First Amendment. It was Flynt's favorite topic, perhaps even more so than sex. The First Amendment was the very thing that brought him here to this Godforsaken little town in Georgia, and he was here to defend himself as well as that first change to the United States Constitution. In fact, he had brought the cavalry with him, determined to prove to these hicks that the definition of "obscenity" was a matter of personal taste, not a punishable crime. It was his right under the umbrella of the First Amendment to print and distribute what he considered to be a mere depiction of human sexuality, and sexuality was anything but a crime.

Flynt was there by design, of course. He had rented out a small store in Gwinnett County named Stan's Shopette for an entire day, selling autographed issues of *Hustler* magazine to customers eager to get their hands on one. In actuality, the magazine was sold in Georgia mostly at small, out-of-the-way newsstands like Stan's, wrapped in brown paper and tucked harmlessly away behind store counters. But to a Southern Baptist, a brown wrapper was a sure sign of the evil hidden within. It didn't matter if the "obscenity" was wrapped in brown paper; everybody knew that magazines in brown paper wrappers were the "devil's publications" and as such, they were not welcome on Southern shelves. The conservatives that ruled the South with an iron fist were not having it. In a *Hustler* magazine article written by Ron Ridenour and entitled "The Shooting of Larry Flynt, Conspiracy Against Truth," Flynt explained that Gwinnett solicitor Gary Davis had sent one of his investigators to the Shopette to buy copies of *Hustler* and *Chic* magazines, then used those copies to levy obscenity charges against him. Solicitor General Hinson McAuliffe of Fulton County did the same thing, which is why Flynt was scheduled to return to Atlanta after the trial in Gwinnett was over. His idea to rent out Stan's Shopette was intentional, a figurative "up yours" to the conservatives and religious leaders who, according to Flynt, had their hand on "society's (collective) crotch." According to the opinionated publisher, as long as the religious right controlled the way society thought about sex, they controlled society. Flynt loved the attention, and he thrived on the controversy. Some said that he sought the limelight because it boosted magazine sales, but Gene Reeves didn't believe that for a minute. Flynt did the outlandish things he did not to peddle porn (porn peddles itself, always has), but because he was passionate about the First Amendment.

Larry Flynt believed that attorneys served a purpose, and God knew he kept his share of them busy, but he didn't have any illusions about the nature of what they did. They were bloodsucking liars and if you paid them enough money, they'd suck someone else's blood instead of yours, at least for a little while.

Bringing in Reeves to help pick the jury was a brilliant decision, a win-win for the entire team. Paul Cambria, Flynt's co-counsel for the trial (and still today, Cambria's firm represents Flynt and his many enterprises), was thrilled to have Reeves on board. The Southern attorney was surprisingly sharp, and having him on board allowed Cambria and skillful co-counsel Herald Fahringer to focus on orchestrating and executing a masterful defense. By all accounts, that's exactly what they were doing. The trial, in Reeves's opinion, was going very well for Flynt. The proceedings, if all continued to go well, were expected to wrap up on Monday, March 6.

Flynt had intentionally pushed the envelope in Georgia so that he could come here to this podunk town to make a point. He wanted to be here, to sit in a courtroom in a small Southern town smack in the middle of the Bible Belt, so that he could crusade for the right to speak freely and openly, no matter how distasteful what he had to say might be to some. He used that right to print the most lewd and lascivious rag Reeves had ever seen, but that just proved his point. "It's not just your speech that ought to be free; it ought to be everyone's," Flynt would tell reporters hanging around the courthouse, news churners hungry to snag a controversial remark from the king of porn. That premise, according to Flynt, was the true test of whether America considered the First Amendment to be a bona fide, God-given right of her citizens. On this one point, Reeves was in full agreement with Flynt.

Reeves was a stickler for the proper execution of the law, right down to the fine points that many religious folks choked on. A person's right under the First Amendment to say or print anything he pleased, no matter how offensive some may have considered it, was one of those fine points. Another was the true definition of "reasonable doubt." "People find themselves in trouble for all kinds of reasons. That doesn't make them bad people," he said years after his retirement, in that same mesmerizing voice that no doubt contributed to his long and respected career. Based on this singular belief, Reeves had fashioned himself into a tough yet charming opponent, with a reputation even among long-time cops for being a dogged cross-examiner. He had loved the law since he was a young boy growing up in Mississippi. He couldn't count the times he'd skipped classes in his small high school and run over to the courthouse to sit in on criminal trials. Whenever he'd read about an upcoming criminal case at the courthouse, he knew that's where he'd be for the duration of the proceedings. His daddy would inevitably hear about his son's absence from school from a teacher or worse, from the principal, and Gene would get an earful from him and Mama when he got home. His parents, a homemaker and a railroad man (a carpenter, really, who built cabooses for the GM&O Railroad) thought their son's fascination with the law was just plain odd. They didn't discourage his pursuit of it; they just didn't want him skipping classes in that pursuit. No one in the family was an attorney, nor were there any police officers that his parents could recall on either side of the family. Neither of them had any idea where their son's preoccupation with the legal system began, or why.

He never cut an entire day of school, just the classes that conflicted with a criminal trial. More than fifty years later, Reeves smiled with a bit of feigned pride when he made that point. Every time a criminal case was being tried in the Lauderdale County courthouse in Meridian, an eager Gene Reeves was right there on the front row. His parents knew it, his teachers knew it, and even the bailiff down at the courthouse knew it. Sometimes, he'd save Gene a seat if the trial was going to be a big one.

Because he loved the law as he did, he could respect what Flynt was trying to do regarding free expression and the First Amendment, but good Lord did he seem to go about it the hard way. Attorneys are taught in law school to show respect to both the courtroom and the presiding judge. "Go along to get along," one of his professors used to say, adding that a good attorney could fight any enemy in a courtroom with skillful technique and proper preparation, except the judge.

Flynt, on the other hand, seemed to prefer bulldozing his way through the courts, ridiculing, flaunting, and taunting, often finding himself behind bars for contempt of those same courts. He was smart though; there was no denying that. Reeves thought that it was sometimes that fact alone that provoked judges, lawyers, and even pastors past the point of reasonable debate. Flynt lacked the tact and finesse, the respectful decorum, that typically characterizes a courtroom trial and its barristers. That was what puzzled Reeves. Frankly, it puzzled Cambria, too, and he had known Flynt a lot longer than Reeves had. Despite his background and chosen profession ("pimping on paper," many called it), Flynt and his wife Althea—herself a stripper when she met Flynt in one of his clubs—had somehow managed to learn how to comport themselves and hold their own with the likes of statesmen and business tycoons, as well as strippers and shadowy, backwoods thugs. Flynt could be respectful and appear to be quite sophisticated when he chose. It was evident, however, that he had nothing but utter contempt for the legal system, for the "moral majority," or for the conservative blue laws that held Georgia and her sister states in a strangling vise grip. It was evident that he considered the men who held that grip on the First Amendment and other rights to be, in fact, the real thugs. Larry Flynt's attorneys billed numerous hours and medicated many pounding headaches precisely because he held those views.

The two men—the flamboyant porn king and the brilliant but unassuming lawyer—sat huddled together at their corner table in the V&J Cafeteria, discussing the trial that, by all accounts, would probably be over soon. Flynt was confident that he would be acquitted, so he was in an exceptionally good mood. He had testified in court that morning, telling judge G. Hughell Harrison and the captivated jury that *Hustler* was "one big put-on, a satire." Was it wrong? Sure it is, he said. But that didn't make it illegal.

The trial had run long; Friday should have been the last day of the proceedings, and it would have been under normal circumstances. But Larry Flynt and "normal" didn't really go hand in hand. When Wardell Pomeroy took the stand for the defense, Reeves was astonished. A pioneer in the research of the human sexual response, the heavy-hitting author was of course an important resource for the defense. If Flynt's team of attorneys could drive home the point that human sexuality was not evil, not a dirty secret to be hidden behind closed bedroom doors, then the rest of the argument made itself. If sexuality was not evil, then it was not a crime. If sexuality was not a crime, how could its photographic depiction be criminal? The accepted research in the Kinsey Report, in Reeves's opinion, would have sufficed nicely. He could hardly believe that Flynt had actually paid Pomeroy and flown him in to testify. The expense had to be staggering.

Then again, this was Larry Flynt. He didn't do anything halfway, and his lifestyle and profession by default meant that he was often in the company of both the famous and the infamous.

Just before the trial began, Ruth Carter Stapleton, a charismatic Southern Baptist and sister of newly elected United States president Jimmy Carter, telephoned Flynt. She said that she was packing her bags, readying herself to make the 350-mile trip from North Carolina to Georgia to testify on his behalf, to vouch for his character in the obscenity trial. She had been Flynt's spiritual advisor for some time by 1978, and she looked forward to telling the judge and jury that Larry Flynt was a born-again Christian, an upstanding man who was welcome in her home at any time, for any reason. Surely her testimony would carry weight with the jury, she explained to her spiritual pupil and notorious king of porn. Flynt had talked her out of making the trip, thanking her and adding that if the matter had been life and death, he would agree with her coming. But since the charge was a simple misdemeanor, Flynt said that he had prayed about the situation and decided that the trip wouldn't be worth risking any negative publicity for her or for her brother. Presidents and pornographers, in public and on record anyway, should not rub elbows. Such behavior didn't sit well with most people, certainly not in the Deep South.

Flynt's team of attorneys, headed up by Fahringer and Cambria, crossed every "t" and dotted every "i" in their eloquent defense of Flynt and his First Amendment rights. In Reeves's opinion, the skilled lawyers had the judge and jury eating out of their hands. They had every onlooker in the courtroom swayed over to Flynt's way of thinking, even stirring a bit of compassion with the retelling of Flynt's humble, deprived beginnings.

His defenders told a tale of a young man born in the mountains of Kentucky who was so ignorant and uneducated that when he ran away from home and joined the army at age fifteen (using a fake birth certificate), he was quickly and honorably discharged under provisions of Section 8, and sent home. The discharge embarrassed Flynt, according to his attorneys, and he became determined to change his circumstances, to educate himself; he knew that change had to begin with education, and education began with reading. Ironically, just like a young James Vaughn had done as a boy in Alabama, Flynt started by reading comic books. He eventually moved on to the great works of literature, and he could discuss them with the most distinguished literary scholars if given the opportunity. Larry Flynt, according to his legal team, was the quintessential example of a self-made man, the very definition of the American dream. Under different circumstances, the audience might have clapped and given a standing ovation when the defense rested but of course, these were not normal circumstances. The jury did not stand and clap, but when the proceedings were recessed for lunch that last day, understanding and compassion were evident on their faces. The trial was going extremely well and by all accounts, the matter would be handed over to the jury this very afternoon.

Reeves wouldn't have admitted this at the outset of the preparation for the trial, but Flynt was, without a doubt, a genius. The man had the mind of a brilliant litigator, with the mouth of a sailor and his thoughts on sex much of the time. It was a strange combination of attributes, but he had parlayed them into a fortune, nonetheless. Reeves didn't have to agree with all of Flynt's notions, but he had to admit that the combination of brilliance, unpredictability, profanity, and sex was working quite well for the man.

He decided to ask him today, while there was still time, something that had been on his mind since the very first time he had met the larger-than-life multi-millionaire. He had to know what it felt like to have all the cars, money, houses, and women he wanted. As the two picked at their lunches and sipped water from clear plastic tumblers, he finally did ask the question, and he had to grudgingly admit that he admired Flynt's answer.

"Well Gene, you can only drive one car at a time, live in one house at a time, and sleep with one woman at a time." Both men looked at each other and smiled, and that was that.

They ate their light meals slowly, the conversation moving from the trial to the weather, to the plans that both men had when the whole mess was finally over. Flynt was facing obscenity charges in Fulton County, as well, so he'd be back in Georgia soon. Reeves would probably go back to his quiet but successful law practice, and life would go on as normal. He sighed aloud at the thought, and Flynt looked at him as if he expected him to explain. When no explanation came, the conversation moved on.

Every now and then, Reeves would nod and mouth a friendly "hello" to another attorney or acquaintance in the popular diner. Of course, most everyone knew him; the V&J was a popular lunch destination for attorneys, judges, and secretaries doing business on the busy town square.

For very different reasons, most people recognized Larry Flynt, as well. Small towns are unique places. Folks around Gwinnett, for the most part anyway, figured that every man put his pants on one leg at a time. No one fawned over the celebrity pornographer, or even shyly asked for his autograph. Flynt was no more treated like a celebrity than anyone else in the diner was. In fact, a woman or two, and of course the preacher from the Baptist church down the road, made a point to cast scandalized glances over their way, or to glare rather than stare at the attorney and his notorious client. There had been quite a lot of gossip around town about Gene Reeves representing the likes of Larry Flynt. Some of the county and city leaders, both political and religious, made no secret of their disapproval. Not everyone, it seemed, believed in fair legal representation or the First Amendment, except as it applied to their own narrow understanding. Nearly forty years after the trial, Reeves would smile and say that his choice to assist Flynt's legal team had certainly garnered him his fifteen minutes of fame. He was also quick to say that he'd be more than happy to give all fifteen of them back in exchange for what they ultimately cost him. Many of the locals never forgot that he vigorously represented an unabashed pornographer, and they let him know it. The decision had cost him a few clients. He believed that it even cost him an elected judgeship or two. In the end, however, he said that he'd have made the same choice all over again if given the opportunity. It was the right thing to do. But no matter, anytime after that trial, when Gene Reeves ran for an elected judgeship, the voters turned him away. "People tend to equate the attorney with the person he's defending, and that linked me to Larry Flynt for the rest of my career," Reeves said. "I guess they believe that in order to defend a person, you have to agree with him."

Reeves was eventually appointed magistrate court judge in Gwinnett County by other county judges, and he retired from that same bench. Up until he died in the summer of 2015, no matter how profoundly the 1978 trial impacted his life, he still loved the law with a deep and reverent passion.

Having finished their lunch and used up almost the entire hour they had to do it, the two men pushed back their chairs and stood. Flynt paid the check, leaving the friendly (and admittedly somewhat starstruck) waitress a handsome tip. Today marked their last day to have lunch together at the V&J and surprisingly, Reeves felt a pang of regret at that. Larry Flynt, this trial, and the duties that came with it had come along at a time in his life when they were a much-needed diversion, a welcome focus. For all of his antics and coarse language and outlandish ideas about things, Larry Flynt was a fascinating man with a single-minded passion about something that mattered, whether folks thought it did or not. Reeves felt as though he had done his part here in Georgia to defend one of the sacred provisions of the US Constitution, the right to express ideas freely. Yes, he would miss the challenge and companionship of these last few weeks. He'd particularly miss their lunches at the V&J. The place had been a favorite of Reeves for years, and Flynt seemed to enjoy the low-key atmosphere and (mostly) friendly patrons. The men liked it so much they had gone there every day for lunch during the trial preparation and the trial itself. It had become their habit, one that a man could set his watch by if he had a mind to.

Attorney and client gathered their overcoats (they certainly wouldn't be needing them for the walk back to the courthouse today), pushed their chairs in, and turned their conversation back to the proceedings as they made their way to the exit. Reeves opened the door for Flynt, and both men stepped out into the bright March sunshine.

CHAPTER 11
Fertile Soil

THERE ARE TWO truths about small Southern towns that people mostly overlook, if they ever see them at all. First, the towns never forget. They laze under summer suns and pull their cloaks tight against freezing winters, all the while soaking up the comings and goings of folks' everyday lives. A small town has a soul of its own, made up of the collective sorrows and joys of its citizens both living and departed—small town secrets and crimes. A small Southern town keeps its soul in the dark, a well-guarded secret. Second, the life of most small Southern towns is a cycle pulsing to a rhythm measured in generations.

Some say these peaks and valleys in the life of a town are natural, nature's way of cleansing and rebirthing, giving and then taking away. They're nature's way of keeping accounts. Others whisper that the bad times are brought on by unspeakable things that have taken place in days gone by, and folks' enduring them is a steep installment payment on a growing debt that will never be fully satisfied. It's also been said that there is blood in the very soil in the South, and that may be true.

Fact and folklore are incestuous lovers though, and no one today can truly tell where one leaves off and the other begins. Children in these parts have whispered the timeworn stories among themselves for hundreds of years, nervously looking over their shoulders and hardly daring to utter the worst of the tales even in secret. Many a terrifying truth has been shared in hushed tones around campfires and under thick bedcovers, truths masked in make-believe, and feigned giggles and gasps. Town elders speak of these same secret things only in the tightest of circles, and the tales are almost always followed by hastily incanted prayers, by favor only God can grant. They pray for protection. They pray for forgiveness.

There are some dark debts that must be paid by those who call a Southern town "home," and very often, they are ultimately paid in blood.

History has graced the southern United States with riches and beauty beyond measure; yet, there are disgraces and infamy from which the region will likely never separate itself. Indecencies wielded by humans against other humans date all the way back to the time that the area was first settled, in an era when proud and peaceable natives lived and thrived in the fertile hills and red clay of Georgia and her neighboring states. The proud Native American nations, mainly Creek and Cherokee, had for years enjoyed a peaceful partnership with settlers that had jostled and elbowed their way into Georgia, Alabama, and Tennessee. The native nations gladly shared their hunting, farming, and survival wisdom with the newcomers. But then greed—that most ugly of the seven deadlies—reared its head and unleashed its voracious appetite on the peaceful hosts.

Early white Georgians began to covet the luscious green hills of north Georgia and the flat, fertile land of the southern region, even then ripe and pregnant with cotton and peanut crops. In time, sharing the abundance to be found here with the people who had welcomed them was not enough for the South's newest inhabitants; the gluttonous settlers wanted it all, and they began driving out the area's oldest inhabitants by any means necessary.

Land cessions, taken by hook or by crook, snowballed until the true native southerners had been thoroughly betrayed, cornered and starving. Laws, treaties, and deals were formed and broken, forcing the natives from their home and farther out onto the harsh frontier to the west. The great Georgia gold rush was the final rusty nail in a coffin that would ultimately entomb thousands of proud, peaceful people. No, the clash between Native Americans and the arrogant settlers pouring in from England did not begin out on the Wild West frontier. It was born in the rich, voluptuous mountains of north Georgia.

By 1837, more than twenty-five million acres of land had been stolen and made available for predominantly white settlement, because forty-six thousand Native Americans from the southeastern states had been removed from their homelands. For a time, the hills truly did run with the blood of innocents; in fact, many a legend attributes the characteristic sticky, blood-red clay of Georgia and her sister states to the wholesale bloodshed that drove out those who had welcomed the newcomers with kindness and civility.

In the fewer than one hundred years between the time that British General James Oglethorpe and his band of debtors first set foot on Georgia soil in the early 1800s, most of the five tribes who had welcomed the settlers had been driven out by brute force and cruel trickery. Tens of thousands more were forced to walk from Georgia to Oklahoma, struggling and dying on the now infamous Trail of Tears. Unceremoniously marked by a bronze plaque in the north Georgia gold mining town of Dahlonega, the trail was drawn out of the politically termed "Cherokee Relocation" and "Indian Removal Act." From 1836 to 1839, thousands of Native Americans were forced to march more than two thousand miles through several states, in a cold effort to relocate them to Oklahoma. No one knows exactly how many died along that grueling migration that lasted three years, but the first round of ethnic cleansing in the southern states is responsible for the deaths of thousands, that much is known, and make no mistake—despair and devastation leave indelible footprints.

The land of a region and its history are inexorably intertwined, as any historian or anthropologist believes wholeheartedly. The story of the South is no different; it can be told simply by exploring the forests, the hills, and the rich earth that comprise it.

When the forced march along the Trail of Tears commenced, legend has it that Cherokee mothers were so grief-stricken that they were unable to help their own children along the way. They were being stripped of a home and a culture deeply rooted in the very land on which they had lived and thrived for many years. Their tears wet the red earth and hardscrabble along the trail, and the tribes' elders prayed for a sign that might lift the mothers' spirits, one that would give them the strength to endure the cruel journey. Tribe elders came together and prayed for peace and comfort for the mothers, enough to sustain them along the exhausting trail that claimed hundreds of lives every day.

The story goes that the morning after the prayer was offered up, a beautiful rose began to grow where each of the mothers' tears had fallen. The flower was white, for the tears that had been shed. It had a gold center, to represent the gold that was stolen from the Cherokee lands. Seven leaves on each stem marked the seven Cherokee clans. The wild Cherokee Rose, as the white flower came to be called, grows all along the route of the Trail of Tears, from Georgia through Alabama, Tennessee, and all the way into eastern Oklahoma still today. Ironically, the state flower of Georgia is the Cherokee Rose.

Interestingly, Lawrenceville, Georgia, was once Creek Indian territory. Tainted soil? Some believe so.

As the 1800s unfolded and cotton reigned supreme on sprawling Southern plantations, the abomination of the slave trade became woven into the fabric of the way of life in the South. European countries and economies had thrived for years on the backs of slaves, many of them captured by fellow Africans and sold to the highest bidders. Thousands of Africans were shipped to the Atlantic coast of the upstart, brash new America. Wealthy plantation owners, who took great pride in their genteel way of life, gave no more thought to selling a slave mother's children away from her than they might have a dog's or a horse's offspring on the market trading block.

The result was then and is even now a deep-rooted hatred and mistrust between many blacks and whites in the region. The scars run painfully deep. At their foundation, they are as raw and visceral today as they were three hundred years ago. Hate is alive and well in the rich, red clay that nourished those cotton plantations so many years ago. It is alive and abundant in the soil that nourishes the Cherokee Rose. Its veins streak the red clay like gold in the north Georgia hills. It was that same soil that nourished a young, angry Joseph Paul Franklin.

The "old rock building" from which Franklin shot Flynt and Reeves (as it looks today). *Photo by Carole Townsend.*

The front door of the old rock building, from which Franklin shot Flynt & Reeves (door used to have a window in it). *Photo by Carole Townsend.*

The historic courthouse in the center of the Gwinnett County town square (in Lawrenceville). The clock atop the building is the one to which I refer when Franklin is staking out the trial and Larry Flynt. *Photo by Carole Townsend.*

Pictured here is Crogan Street, part of the town square (as it looked about fifty years ago). The county square was the crown jewel of Gwinnett County. Today, it boasts lofts and retail shops. The courthouse is now an historic building that houses the Gwinnett Historical Society, and in which weddings are performed at no charge by judges every Valentine's Day. The courthouse is a popular venue for weddings throughout the year. *Photo courtesy of the Lawrenceville Police Department.*

Klan marchers demonstrate in Gwinnett County. The Klan remained openly active in Gwinnett County, as recently as the 1980s. *Photo courtesy of the Lawrenceville Police Department.*

A KKK march coming down Perry Street in the early 1980s. The officer in the forefront is standing in front of the old rock building. *Photo courtesy of the Lawrenceville Police Department.*

Klansmen meet/rally in town square in the early 1980s. *Photo courtesy of the Lawrenceville Police Department.*

Gwinnett County built a $72 million Justice and Administration Center in 1988. Pictured here: A Klansman demonstrates at the new state-of-the-art facility. *Photo courtesy of the Lawrenceville Police Department.*

Photo courtesy of the Lawrenceville Police Department.

Photo courtesy of the Lawrenceville Police Department.

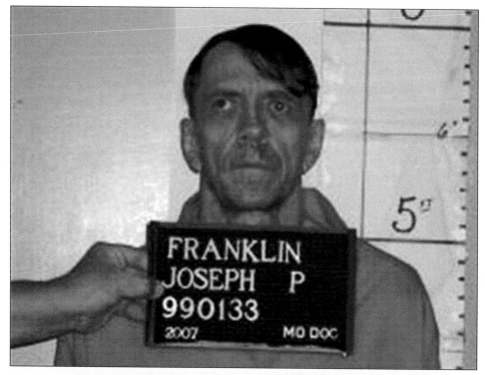

Franklin's 2007 booking photo, Missouri Department of Corrections.

Det. Michael Cowart in 1981. *Photo courtesy of the Lawrenceville Police Department.*

Frank "Mac" McKelvey and (ret) Lawrenceville police chief Bill Dean. *Photo courtesy of the Lawrenceville Police Department.*

Carl White, Michael Cowart, and Frank McKelvey. *Photo courtesy of the Lawrenceville Police Department.*

Photo of the GCPD officers at the old police headquarters in the late '70s/early '80s. Front row far right is police chief Crunkleton. *Photo courtesy of the Lawrenceville Police Department.*

(L-R) M.J.Puckett, Lawrenceville PD Chief J.O. Bell, Bryant Huff, Jake Roberts, and John Paul Harris. Huff was the District Attorney of Gwinnett County when Flynt and Reeves were shot, and when Franklin confessed to the shootings. *Photo courtesy of the Lawrenceville Police Department.*

CHAPTER 12
Blood and Justice

IF ANY OF the busy people in the town square down below him happened to glance up at the windows on the top floor of the rock building around 11:30 that morning, they might have seen a gaunt, predatory face looking back at them. There was no doubt that they would have remembered that face. But they *wouldn't* see him, because he was a ghost, an apparition. That's why he'd been able to execute his crusade for more than a year now, and that's why he knew that he would succeed in his mission today. Contemplating that thought, he turned and made his way back down the narrow hallway, down the stairs, and back to the front door of the building. It was almost time.

He couldn't believe his luck. When he had read in the newspaper that Flynt's obscenity trial would take place in Lawrenceville, Georgia, he wasn't even sure where that was. As it turned out, Lawrenceville was just a short drive straight up I-85 North from the Days Inn Motel where he had been staying when he first read about the trial. Just one more sign that God sent him, affirming his mission to rally whites in this country to take back what was theirs. When he read about the trial, he checked out of the Days Inn and checked into the Golfland Motel, a little farther to the south. He was always moving; there, and then not.

About a week ago, Franklin had brought in the green burlap and tacked it above the glass on the front door. No one had even noticed, because it was still here, undisturbed. *Because people are stupid, like fucking sheep.* The makeshift curtain would hide any movement he'd make from the view of possible onlookers passing by on Perry Street. He had thought of every detail.

Being careful not to be seen by some nosy pedestrian, Franklin leaned closer to the dirty glass and looked up and down Perry Street. Backing slowly away from the door, he reached down to check the gun one more time. The stolen .44 Marlin rifle was a gun powerful enough to knock back and probably kill an elephant from this distance, but that wasn't why he chose it. Because he was almost completely blind in his right eye, Franklin had taught himself to shoot left-handed. He was an excellent marksman despite his handicap. Since bolt-action rifles are made for right-handed shooters, the Marlins and Winchesters, with their slant action levers, had become a favorite tool of his trade. The barrel of a Marlin rifle is short, making it easy to transport and handle. Hunters called it a "brush gun," since it was easier to carry through thick brush and woods than a longer gun would be. It was a louder gun than he preferred, but it was a powerful weapon and today, he would make a powerful statement. The loud noise of such a firearm sometimes actually worked in his favor, as that's what people tended to remember after a shooting. It was always the same: "I thought it was a truck backfiring," or something like that. They saw his real handiwork well after he had left the scene, and that was all right by him.

If he were planning to shoot Flynt at night, he wouldn't have chosen this gun. The Marlin would sometimes throw fire out the end of the barrel, and an unusual sight like that here on the town square would not do. A flash in the night would quickly give away his position, and would also give folks something to remember. Fire was something that passersby always noticed. *Quick in and out. Smooth. Invisible.* Just like he had rehearsed, and played out, so many times before.

Facing the middle of the room, he held the gun up to his left shoulder, squinted as he looked down the slick barrel, and made a slight clicking sound as he pretended to pull the trigger. Satisfied that the sights were lined up and straight, he carefully leaned the gun against the wall, closed his eyes, and began the ritual, the one he performed before several murders he'd committed. He had to see it all in his mind before he ever made a move. No mistakes. No surprises. He'd have to clear his mind, and for Joseph Franklin, that was difficult. A clear mind left room for memories to come flooding in.

The young boy sat quietly in the waiting room, gingerly touching the patch that covered his eye and waiting for his mother to finish talking to the doctor. The injury was a bad one, but according to the doctor, it did not have to be permanent. "Be sure you bring him back for the surgery, Mrs. Vaughn. We have to let the eye heal for a few weeks, and after that, the operation will take care of the rest." He heard his mother promise to bring her son back, and then she and the doctor emerged from the examination room. The doctor tousled the little boy's hair and reassured him. "You're going to be just fine, young man. We'll see you in a couple of weeks." And that was the last time that Jimmy Vaughn ever saw the kind doctor. Helen Vaughn never again mentioned an operation or any other treatment for her son's eye. He maybe hated her most for that.

His hands tightened as the stinging memory washed over the other thoughts in his head, and he willed himself to regain control. *Calm. Smooth. Quiet. In and out, just like always.* He took deep and measured breaths, concentrating on the mission before him. He leaned back against the wall and slid all the way down until he touched the floor, where he folded his legs and sat cross-legged. Reaching into his shirt pocket and fishing out a crumpled pack of Marlboros, he reviewed every step he had planned before he actually carried out the mission. *Wait. Take aim. Shoot. No quick movements. Out the back. Down the alley to the car. Then just hang a right and drive.* Simple. He had completed much more complicated missions during his young crusade, but none as important as this one.

The waiting was the hardest part. Always was. He shook a cigarette out of the pack, struck a match against the dusty wood floor, and lit it. Dragging deep on the cigarette, he filled his lungs with the harsh smoke, then slowly exhaled. *Calm.* He tried not to think about his mother, her hate and neglect. He tried not to think about the revolting mixed race couple in the magazine, doing things that even animals wouldn't do, but the images stubbornly played and flickered across his mind just the same. It wasn't right. *Whites with whites. Blacks with blacks. Jews with Jews. Orientals with Orientals. That's what God intended.* Anything else was just blasphemy and degradation. When he thought about it that way, there was really no other course of action. Get rid of Larry Flynt, get rid of *Hustler* magazine. *Cut off the head, and the body will die.* It was a beautifully simple, inspired plan.

The regal clock atop the county courthouse began ringing out the hour for the benefit of all who could hear it: straight up twelve o'clock. Just a few minutes before that, as Reeves and Flynt were finishing their salads at their customary corner table in the V&J, Reeves asked a question of his client that had been on his mind throughout the trial. He wanted to know what it was like to be Larry Flynt, to have everything he wanted and more. While the clock chimed, both men were smiling at Flynt's matter-of-fact response. As the men rose and made their way to the diner's exit, the conversation turned back to the obscenity trial and its likely favorable outcome. Both men were confident as they opened the door and stepped out into the uncharacteristically bright March sunshine.

The rich tones of the bells snapped Franklin out of his reverie. He snuffed out what was left of his cigarette on the floor, flicked the butt onto the growing pile in the corner, and then wiped his hands on his pants. *Time to get to work.*

Rolling onto his hands and knees, he crawled over to the window and pulled back the burlap curtain just enough to get a good look at the sidewalk across the street, down by the V&J. There were people walking, all right, but he didn't see Flynt and Reeves among them. *I didn't miss them. I couldn't have.* Just the night before, Joe himself had dined at the V&J, and he had walked the same route that Flynt and Reeves had walked several times, from the cafeteria back to the courthouse. He knew exactly how long it took. Rolling to his left, away from the window, he crossed his legs again and placed his hands on his head, rubbing the bristled hair and taking slow and measured breaths. Pushing down irritation that might easily mushroom into full-blown panic, Franklin began going over the plan again, step by step. Just doing that calmed him, as it always did. He eased over to the window and raised up slightly, so as to take another look.

Walking along the sidewalk almost directly across from his hiding place, suit jackets unbuttoned and flapping slightly in the breeze, were Gene Reeves and Larry Flynt. A magazine reporter and another man trailed the pair, shadowing them even as they took a break from the court proceedings. The warm sunshine was flirting with both gentlemen, with everybody out there, in fact. People were smiling, the kind of smiles that only a warm day at the tail end of winter can bring. The two men were walking slowly, and they seemed to be engulfed in deep conversation. *Good.*

Franklin carefully got to his feet, then reached down for the Marlin, never taking his eyes off the two men as they walked back to the courthouse on Pike Street. His fingertips just brushed the tip of the barrel, and the rifle fell to the floor beside him. The barrel scraped along the wall before the weapon hit the wood floor, bouncing and clattering as it did. Wincing at the noise, sure someone had heard the clanging and rattling as the gun hit the bare floor, Franklin closed his eyes and froze. His window of opportunity was closing—slamming shut, in fact—and he knew it. *It's now or never.* Going down on one knee and grabbing the Marlin up in the same movement, he raised the gun to his left shoulder, lowered his head a bit, closed his right eye, and got a bead on his target. His finger twitched on the trigger, and he switched his focus from Larry Flynt to his index finger, studying it, willing it to stop shaking. *Not yet. Not too soon. You need a clean shot.* His gaze returned to Gene Reeves and, more importantly, to his client, both men strolling through the mottled shade on Perry Street as they made their way back to the state courthouse. The two were almost even with the old rooming house now. In a few seconds, their backs would be to him. He'd never get a better chance. He found Flynt again and took aim with the powerful Marlin, squinted with his good eye through the calibrated sight on the barrel, and followed him. *Now. Now.*

Joseph Paul Franklin jacked the lever on the gun and pulled the trigger in one practiced motion, shooting Larry Flynt as he walked back to the state courthouse to defend his right to free speech and redefine for Georgia the word "obscenity." The bullet grazed Flynt and ricocheted into Reeves's arm, then his spleen, liver, and pancreas, and then his gall bladder, where it exploded. The target had stopped walking and was looking at Reeves, who was lying in the street. The expression on Flynt's face was puzzlement, disbelief. He could not reconcile what he was seeing with everything else that was happening around him. The sun was shining, the birds were singing, a fresh breeze played with his hair and with his tie, and his attorney and lunch companion was lying in the street, moaning and bleeding, trying to pull himself to safety behind a parked car. Something about the scene wasn't right; he just couldn't put his finger on it.

Franklin jacked the Marlin's lever again, expelling a spent cartridge onto the dusty floor, and took careful aim. He pulled the trigger and with the second shot, he hit Flynt in the lower back, knocking him forward four or five feet before he fell to the ground.

The confused expression had left Flynt's face; in its place were pain and shock. He stared, unblinking, into the brilliant blue sky, muttering "What happened?" Black blood bloomed and spread across his abdomen, and it pooled underneath him. Reeves, who had been wounded in Korea years earlier, answered him. "We've been shot."

From the time he first spotted the men to taking the second shot at them, about thirty seconds had elapsed. As always though, it seemed to Franklin like it had been a lot longer. He stared out at his handiwork, relishing that sweet spot in time between the shooting and the reaction of the crowd, no matter how close or how far away they might have been at the time that they heard the (truck backfiring? pallets dropping? gunshot?) sound. In that split second, there is pure, sweet silence while the sheep are trying to register what just happened before their very eyes. In that narrow slice of time, Franklin always felt his best, the closest he ever came to feeling truly happy. Those few seconds were like looking at a painting that he, the artist, had finally finished.

A .44 Marlin is built for business, not pleasure. Seasoned hunters have shared fireside stories of taking down charging grizzly bears with a single shot using the stocky, powerful weapon. The devastation that Franklin wrought that beautiful Monday afternoon in March 1978 would not be fully grasped by the victims, the media, or the medical community for some time.

Gene Reeves, who despite his injuries saw that Flynt had been hit badly, tried to struggle to his feet to render aid to his client. He never lost consciousness; nearly forty years later, the events of that day replayed clearly for the retired attorney and magistrate judge.

After the shooting, Flynt lay prone on the ground, right next to a lovely bed of buttercups and tulips, staring into nothingness, clearly in shock, and clutching his now-exposed insides. "Somebody help me. Please," he moaned repeatedly.

Across the way at the state courthouse, Paul Cambria was talking on a pay phone outside the state court building, looking directly at Reeves and Flynt when he heard two loud cracks. He saw the men drop, as if they had hit an invisible wall while strolling along Perry Street in the warming sunshine. Dropping the phone mid-sentence and running to the scene, he shouted, "Larry! They shot Larry!" That's when the window slammed shut on Joseph Franklin's beloved sweet spot.

The cheerful spring flowers that bloomed along the sidewalk were splattered with the blood of both men. Blood was on the sidewalk, on the telephone pole that the men were walking past when they were hit, and on Perry Street itself, the sun shining down on the whole mess and giving the scene a garish, unrealistic patina.

Two men ran to the bloody scene, crouched down, and began to talk to Gene Reeves and the infamous pornography king, who for all they knew were going to die right there on the town square, before God and all these people. One of the men first on the scene, Reeves recalled later, was Hill Jordan, another attorney after whose family Rhodes Jordan Park over on East Crogan Street is named today. He did not hesitate to do what he could to comfort the men, even though he was familiar with Flynt and his scandalous reputation.

The other man who rushed to the scene was pastor Fred Musser; he knelt beside Flynt and encouraged him to hang on until help arrived, assuring him that he was going to be all right, trying to soothe the fears of the panicked man who was slipping quickly into deep shock.

A crowd started gathering but oddly, only a few approached the actual scene of the shooting where the two men lay bleeding in the street. In one of many strange twists of luck to come, Lawrenceville police chief Bobby Plunkett happened to drive right up on the scene as soon as the shooting happened. He was able to ascertain almost immediately that the shots must have come from the direction of the old rock building, based on the apparent angle from which the force hit Flynt. The second powerful shot had knocked him four, maybe five feet off of the course the men were walking. Bystanders couldn't be sure where the shots had come from, or even whether what they had heard were gunshots. Officer Michael Cowart, then a beat cop, was radioed to the scene of the shooting (Lawrenceville was, after all, his beat), but he was busy directing traffic around a brush fire north of the area, in the Hamilton Mill area of the county.

A few years down the road, that same cop—who by then would be a seasoned and shrewd Detective Michael Cowart—would emerge as the lead investigator on the case. There would come a time when Cowart would become the person who probably knew Joseph Franklin better than anyone ever had, not because Franklin willingly revealed himself, but because Cowart got a front-row seat to the tragedy that was Joe Franklin and his life. What he learned about the man is still quite fresh in his memory, and some of it still haunts him today.

A block over, rookie officer Tom Medley's radio crackled with the directive from Gwinnett County Police Dispatch to shut down all traffic passing on Clayton Street. Less than ten seconds earlier, a green 1972 Ford Gran Torino had passed right by him, headed straight out of Lawrenceville toward Scenic Highway, on a deliberate path south. Medley had been on the job for about two weeks when Gene Reeves and Larry Flynt were shot. Now retired, he can still recall the day's events as though they had happened just yesterday.

Later that afternoon, eyewitnesses would report seeing two men speeding off in a pickup truck right after the shots were fired. Still others would swear they saw a man throw a pistol out the passenger side window of a car of unidentified make and model. Others swore they saw a black and silver Chevrolet Camaro speed away from the square not long after the shots were fired. Some said the getaway car was an El Camino, and it was driven by a wild-haired black man. *You can always count on the sheep for help.*

Over on Perry Street, officers who had arrived on the scene began securing the area, all the while looking up into the windows of the surrounding buildings. Two officers were rolling out the yellow crime scene tape. Sirens screamed in the distance, wailing louder as they got closer. The chaos multiplied by the minute.

Franklin relished as much of the aftermath of his handiwork as he had dared before making his rehearsed exit. *Two shots. Damn. Sight must've gotten knocked off kilter when the gun fell. Well, no use crying over spilt milk*, as his mother used to say. He rose to his feet and, slipping the gun back into the white pillowcase, simply turned and walked to the back door of the rock building. He opened it (it didn't stick this time) and looked both left and right before stepping out onto the concrete landing. Seeing no one running toward him, he jogged down the back stairs of the building. At the bottom of the stairs, he leaned over and looked into the alley that led to Perry Street, glancing first left, then right. There were people, all right, but they were all running to the spot where Reeves and Flynt lay in the street. Not one person was looking in his direction and even if they had been, they probably wouldn't have really noticed him, amidst the chaos.

Walking swiftly but being careful not to look hurried, Franklin crossed the parking lot, opened the squeaky door on the driver's side of the Gran Torino, and slid into the seat. He pitched the Marlin onto the back seat, started the ignition, shifted into DRIVE, and exited the parking lot. He turned right onto Clayton Street, which officer Medley would be closing down tighter than a drum in a few seconds, and rolled right on out of town, just as pretty as you please. A quick glance into his rearview mirror revealed a sea of flashing blue lights and a gathering crowd. Cops scrambled this way and that, going about the meticulous business of trying to figure out what the hell had just happened.

As soon as he was clear of Lawrenceville and all the hullaballoo he left behind, he stopped at the Phillips 66 service station and made his call to the state courthouse.

In all the years since the shooting, the gun that Joseph Paul Franklin used that day to shoot Larry Flynt and Gene Reeves has never been found. By his own account, he "busted the stock off" the rifle and threw it into a Dumpster somewhere along the interstate as he headed south in Georgia. Later, he sawed the barrel into several pieces, burying them in a secret location under a bridge near Grady hospital in Atlanta—an old survival trick he learned from his idol, Joseph Goebbels. The pieces have never been found.

CHAPTER 13
Dancing with the Devil
(1983)

Detective Michael Cowart

The three of us stood there in that tiny cell, Mac and I opposite one another and Franklin in the middle, his right hand fully extended for a handshake, his left hanging awkwardly mid-air. Before he invited the handshake, he had bent over and placed a small box underneath the chair closest to him. We were curious, but not concerned. Any box that he had been allowed to bring to this meeting had been screened by at least a dozen guards, of that we could be certain.

The chains that snaked around his wrists, then his waist, and then his ankles, necessitated the odd posture. Our positioning in the room was no accident; we had thoroughly studied the FBI profiler's report that had been provided to us several weeks ago, when we arranged this meeting to hear what Franklin had to say about the Gwinnett County shooting five years ago. There was no clock on the wall either, though I imagine that was always the case. A hardened "lifer" could build a bomb, a knife, probably even a garden shed or a Ferris wheel from the pieces he could remove from a plain old wall clock.

Although it was an awkward motion, I shook Franklin's hand just as I would a friend's, and Mac did the same. Franklin did the best he could with the gesture, then we all pulled up a chair to the round metal table, which had been anchored to the ground in the center of the room. We settled back into our seats to begin the conversation (or the "dance," as I would come to think of this and any future conversations I had with Franklin).

I'll never forget the first time I saw Joe (he continued to insist that I call him Joe, though he didn't seem to care what Mac called him). He was slender, but tightly muscled. He wore wire-rimmed glasses, and his head was clean-shaven. He had several crude tattoos that were visible, but not nearly as many as a lot of the inmates had. On one arm was a morbid drawing of the grim reaper; for some reason, that is the tattoo that I remember most clearly.

At that first visit back in '83, Franklin still looked pretty healthy. He was a bit smaller than Mac and me, but it was obvious that he exercised as much as he could, given the tight security measures in the special unit that was now his home. Still I thought, *This is it? This is the legendary Joseph Paul Franklin? He sure doesn't look like much.* In my experience though, no matter how heinous the crime, the criminal never seems to live up to what the imagination conjures.

Once we were left alone, the two lawmen and the prisoner sized one another up quickly and efficiently. Probably the only thing the three of us had in common was our ability to evaluate others with uncanny speed and accuracy. The conversation began, once formalities were over, with an empty observation about the weather, or what Franklin could glimpse of it whenever the chance arose. We followed suit, playing along as we continued to evaluate body language and eye contact. It was rather uncomfortable, trying to establish and maintain eye contact with Joe across that small table. His damaged right eye, which was for all practical purposes blind, peered in a slightly different direction than his left eye. After a few more trivial exchanges about sports and the weather, I steered the conversation to meatier matters, like why we had been summoned from Georgia to Illinois to meet with a man serving two life sentences for multiple murders. I could think of at least one place on every continent I'd rather have been than sitting there in that claustrophobic room, across the table from this very twisted man.

Despite my efforts, Franklin tried to deftly steer the conversation to, of all topics, the 1983 baseball playoffs. I stopped him at that point, bringing the conversation back around to the 1978 shooting. He smiled, then began complaining about the food that was served to prisoners at Marion. I stopped him again and read him his Miranda rights. "I know you've heard this before, but bear with me. It's for your protection, Joe."

You must remember that, by the time we actually shook hands with one another, Joe Franklin and I had corresponded by mail a few times. During those communications, we had developed the façade of a friendship, or so it appeared. In truth, I was trying to build a thin veneer that looked like friendship. That appearance was crucial to any investigation that might result. At no time did I ever consider Joe Franklin a friend, and I have no illusions that he considered me to be one, either, save for the possibility that he might at some point use our "friendship" to get me to lower my guard, so that he could again escape custody. The bare fact of the matter is that we were both using each other for something. I wanted information, and he wanted to get out of Marion. I had been tasked with gaining his trust; I do not know how much of a friend Joe ever really considered me to be. For that matter, he himself may not have known, as he had so few such relationships to which he could compare ours.

Joe listened to his Miranda rights, nodding every now and then, until I finished with the familiar, "Do you understand these rights as they have been read to you?" Yes, he nodded. He understood. The small talk behind us, Franklin wove a strange, disjointed tale of sorts, one with gaping holes, hinting at crimes he may have committed from Georgia to Tennessee to Wisconsin. His accounts were laced with passionate rants about his hatred of blacks and Jews, so much so that at times, it seemed that he had a hard time remembering what he had been saying. He said that he had critical information about the Larry Flynt shooting. He all but confessed to several bank robberies, shootings, and bombings, crimes that the FBI suspected him of committing, but so far anyway, they couldn't prove it. Or hadn't. And that was the problem. There was the catch. There was the reason we were sitting here in this awful, suffocating place with a killer.

Franklin wanted to talk to the FBI about these crimes, but the FBI refused to talk to him initially. He offered to confess to several unsolved crimes, including bank robberies and bombings, and still they refused. It was a fact that, frankly, puzzled the other Gwinnett detectives and me over the months, though we were happy to benefit from his willingness to talk to us. We could only assume that the Feds didn't take him seriously.

We were, of course, keenly interested in anything Franklin might have to say about the Flynt shooting; it happened, after all, in our jurisdiction, but helping to solve all of the other major crimes Franklin had touched on would be a bonus. Making sure that he would never again be a free man was of critical importance. He was without a doubt the most dangerous man I had ever encountered. And I will say again, the truth of the thing was always what mattered to me. I wanted to know who shot Flynt and Reeves. I wanted to know who bombed the Chattanooga synagogue and a Maryland residence the year before that shooting. The truth was always the thing that motivated me.

We had read enough about this man to know that the FBI definitely had him on their radar (though they might have not been talking to Franklin directly at the time, they had begun to talk to those who knew of him). We had read enough to know that, according to Franklin's dossier, he was suspected of several murders and other crimes, some of which I just mentioned. The FBI had drawn tentative conclusions, but none that were solid.

In a national meeting held in Cincinnati about a year before our meeting with him, Franklin was loosely tied to so many bombings, shootings, and bank robberies that the conference had been called solely in his honor. It was clear to Mac and me that we were dealing with a skilled and rather accomplished bank robber, if nothing else. Robbing banks was how he funded both his lifestyle and his crusade, and he was very good at it.

It was becoming obvious to us that Franklin was frustrated—not quite desperate, but frustrated that the FBI wouldn't give him the time of day. He considered himself to be a pretty big fish, and as it turned out, he was. So why the cold shoulder from the FBI?

Here, then, a new step was incorporated into the dance. Franklin had an ego; we had been advised of that likelihood when we read the psychological assessment, and there it was. And as with any personality trait, a subject's ego is a weakness of sorts; it can be used.

We understood what was going on in that small, austere room deep inside the belly of Marion; Franklin was giving us just enough information about unsolved crimes to whet our appetites, but for what? And then, without any fanfare or warning, Franklin said, "I want out of here. They're trying to kill me."

"Who's trying to kill you, Joe?" I asked.

"Mike Thevis. And the people working for him."

We had known about an attack on Franklin in his early days at Marion, when he was allowed to be among the general population. A group of black inmates had cornered him and stabbed him fifteen or sixteen times before the guards could break up the fray. After that incident, he had been moved to the special holding unit for his own safety and as an extra measure to prevent an escape attempt (always a good idea where Joe was concerned).

Thevis was an interesting character, an Atlanta millionaire who stood accused of using arson, murder, and racketeering to build an empire of adult bookstores and X-rated movie theaters. He was also an inmate at Marion, living in the same quarters as Franklin. He was serving his time there after being convicted of racketeering and conspiring to murder a government witness. That last part is the reason he was housed with the other very bad apples at Marion.

"He's trying to kill me. Here," Franklin whispered, as he reached under his chair to retrieve the small box. We both leaned forward to see what it contained. It was a box of chocolate candy, a slit in the thin protective covering over it.

"He's been giving me candy. He knows I like it. I think it's poisoned. I want you to take it and get it tested by the FBI. You'll see. I'm afraid for my life in here."

On the heels of that accusation, Franklin then told us that Warden Miller was a Jew, and that Miller was part of a conspiracy against him.

Yes, there we had it. He wanted out of Marion. It was as simple as that. Who could blame him, really? It was an imposing, unpleasant place, and I was just a visitor there. I couldn't imagine living out the rest of my life there. Then again, I had never killed a man just because his skin color was different from mine, either. I had never bombed a place of worship, or laid low in the grass like a spineless snake so that I could ambush and murder innocent people.

During the four hours that we met, Mac and I allowed Franklin to ramble on about his strange beliefs. He went into great detail about the "Khazars," the people whom he (and some others) referred to as Jews, and the fact that they were from the mountainous regions of central Europe. According to Franklin, the "Khazars" had usurped us, the original, rightful Jews chosen by God. In his view, they had ousted and oppressed the true Jews, and that is why he hated them. He had brought a pamphlet to our meeting along with the box of candy, and he gave it to me as he preached, so that I could read it and better understand his views. It was clear that today was just a test for him. He wanted to see whether he could manipulate his way out of Marion and into a lower-security prison. His rants were disjointed and disturbing, but they surely gave us a window into who Joseph Franklin was and why he had turned like a rabid dog, and at such a very young age. During this meeting and as a result of our earlier communications, I can say that Joe Franklin was relatively well spoken, though he did stumble at times over grammar.

I can also say without reservation that he was very intelligent, and nobody's fool. That intelligence and his ability to put people at ease, worked together to make him a very dangerous man, indeed.

When the four-hour meeting was over, all three of us stood. At the sound of movement, the small window in the cell door slid open, and a watchful eye surveyed the room. Mac and I both signaled that everything was fine, and the window quietly closed. We could hear the guard unlocking the door, the sound signaling to all three of us that we were finished, at least for today. We were leaving, and I promised to have the candy tested for traces of poison as soon as possible. A second guard had come to the cell to escort us through several checkpoints and ultimately, to our waiting car. Franklin would be escorted back to his cell separately.

After the departing formalities had been addressed between Warden Miller and us (papers had to be signed and statements sworn to), we were escorted to the first perimeter gate, buzzed out, and then escorted to our rented vehicle. We would fly back to Atlanta tomorrow morning, and both of us were too keyed up to go straight back to the hotel. We opted for a late dinner out instead. Lowe, who had been waiting at the hotel during our strange but intriguing meeting, joined us.

Over three rare steaks and as many stiff drinks, Mac and I discussed the events of the day. Both of us had taken notes, but there really hadn't been a need. We had come away from that bizarre four-hour monologue both wary and encouraged. Not only had Joe charged that living conditions at Marion were inhumane, but also he told us that he wanted to be transferred to a place that wasn't run by "niggers and Jews." Of course, he also confided that he feared for his life at the hands of Mike Thevis, whom Franklin alleged had been hired by Flynt to kill him. Yes, Franklin wanted out of Marion very badly. That desire gave us a bargaining chip. Oh of course we would dance again a time or two, but he would soon learn that we would not swallow information as "fact" simply because he told it to us. He would come to see that he'd have to give us facts before he could even hope to try to parlay them into his gain. We may have appeared to him at first to be good old boys just trying to close a cold case file, but we were not. The two-time escapee knew that there was not a chance in hell of escaping from Marion. Even if he could make it as far as the first perimeter, which was next to impossible, he would be shot there in his tracks. His only hope was a transfer to another prison, and that gave us a great deal of leverage.

Later that night, as I lay in my uncomfortable hotel bed with sleep hours away, I pondered the impact of what Franklin had intimated: "*I have knowledge of a case in which he may be interested.*"

The Larry Flynt shooting? Is it really possible? Five years without as much as a single clue, and he's just going to hand himself over like that? And there I was, the man who had always wanted to play "cops and robbers," turning the murderer's words over and over in my mind. I may have joined the police force years ago as a hobby of sorts, something to keep me busy after retiring from the Navy, but over the years I had grown to both love and hate the work. I had done everything from directing traffic to flying airplanes, from working vice to working homicides, even working cold-case murders. I had seen up close the dark side of the human race, there was no doubt about that. I had spent a lot of time with petty criminals and notorious masterminds, more time than I had spent with my own wife, truth be told. I hated that world, but oh how I loved to right the wrongs, or to try to, at least. How I loved to finally lay bare the truth. And I had learned a long time ago that in order to do so, you had to dance the dance, and sometimes, your dance partner was the devil himself.

My mettle, my patience, my skill as an officer of the law would never be tested by anyone as much as Joseph Paul Franklin would test it. I suspected, too, that today's meeting was not the end of it; rather, today was just the start of a long and drawn-out dance with many complicated steps. As it turned out, I was right about that, too.

Right there, in that too-soft bed in that hotel room in Marion, Illinois, I resolved to do the one thing that I knew would gain Franklin's confidence. As soon as I got back to Georgia, I would be sending a half-eaten box of candy to the FBI lab up north, to see whether the candy had been tainted with poison. I felt sure that the answer was "no," but I knew that going through those motions would go a long way toward gaining Franklin's trust. I'd also do what I could to get the *Gwinnett Daily News* sent to the prison in Marion, to Franklin's attention if at all possible. He had asked for that favor at some point during the meeting, saying that he liked to keep up with the goings-on in that little town for some reason. It was a twisted game, but it was one I was willing to play. I was good at playing it. In the long run, both of us proved to be worthy opponents, but only one of us would emerge the victor.

CHAPTER 14
Smoke, Mirrors, and Conspiracies
(1978)

THE MELEE THAT followed the ambush-style shooting of Larry Flynt and Gene Reeves was multi-layered, and it only grew more complicated as the weeks and months passed. The media, already camped outside the courthouse in Gwinnett because of the obscenity trial and its flashy defendant, called in reinforcements following the shooting. Who would do such a thing, and in broad daylight in a busy little town? Had it been a contract killing? Perhaps a religious fanatic had taken it upon himself to cut down Flynt, who they saw as a foul-mouthed sex peddler, before he could gain any more ground in what many perceived to be a clear fight between good and evil. Some had even put forth the notion that the actual target had been Gene Reeves, but no one in his right mind bought that theory, even for a minute. There were those who believed that a white supremacy group, perhaps the Klan, had ordered Flynt's execution. There was good reason to draw that conclusion. The Klan had been very clear on its opinion of Larry Flynt, *Hustler*, pornography, and race-mixing. Shortly after the December 1975 spread ran in *Hustler*, the magazine printed this "Letter to the Editor" in a later issue:

"We write to inform you of our absolute disgust with your magazine. HUSTLER is a complete disgrace to the moral fiber of Caucasian Civilization. Think—we as a nation and race have advanced to the point where we produce, as well as allow sale of, such utter trash. We are referring to the 'Black Stud and His Georgia Peach' feature in your December 1975 issue. No wonder you talk of your periodical's difficulty in obtaining advertisers! We most certainly would not post an ad with you; we have more class than to degrade ourselves to your gutter level of degeneracy.

"We seriously doubt that you will have the courtesy to print this letter, for from your apparent caliber it is to be expected that you will not. Just remember that this nation was not built by cheap women, whore-mongers and race-mixers, but instead by hard-working Christian Caucasians."

The letter was signed by the National Southern Knights of the Ku Klux Klan, Realm of Georgia, Fayette Kounty Klavern.

The flamboyant porn baron was a hated man in some circles. Speculation about who had tried to kill him was the order of the day, and Larry Flynt led the charge on that front, posing several juicy conspiracies as possible reasons for the brutal attack.

In the days immediately following the shooting, Judge G. Hughell Howell (Hughell, to those who knew him) declared a mistrial in light of the unusual circumstances. There was a rumor circulating, one that persists among some even today, that Howell declared the mistrial in exchange for Flynt paying all of Reeves's medical bills that resulted from the attack. Flynt did that, but Reeves and those who knew him well believe that he did so because he felt that it was the decent thing to do, not because of a back room deal made with a judge.

As for Flynt, he only spent a couple of days in Button Gwinnett Hospital following the incident. His abdominal artery had been severed, and he was losing blood at an alarming rate. Dr. Taher Bagheri, the thoracic surgeon whose skill is credited with saving both Reeves's and Flynt's lives in those early hours, removed six feet of Flynt's intestines, but the blood loss still did not stop. Bagheri had to perform two surgeries on Flynt within hours of each other, with troublesome bleeding from his spleen necessitating the second procedure. Dr. Bagheri, who still lives in Gwinnett County and retired from his medical practice in the year 2000, recalls that Larry Flynt was a very good patient while in his care.

Althea Flynt, on the other hand, was a handful. Racked with fear and dread after her husband's shooting, she never left the hospital once she arrived. She spent much of that time with Bagheri while Flynt was in the hospital in Gwinnett, urging him to do more and raining an endless barrage of questions on the exhausted surgeon.

"He stayed in touch, sending me a Christmas card every year for many years," Bagheri said of his famous patient, and he smiled at the memory. As he worked tirelessly to save the men's lives, Bagheri had no idea that the man who had inflicted the injuries was circling the hospital parking lot, plotting to finish what he had begun by shooting Flynt. "I figured I'd just go in to his hospital room and finish him off with a pistol," Franklin recalled more than thirty years later, as he spoke with journalist Beth Karas eight days before his execution. But the always-present swarm of reporters and lawmen discouraged Franklin from finishing his work, and he decided to leave well enough alone, never setting foot in the small hospital.

Flynt was given a total of twenty-four blood transfusions as a result of his injuries, but his physicians knew that he would not survive long unless the bleeding was stopped. Once Bagheri had finished his work in Gwinnett, a medevac helicopter transported Flynt to Emory Hospital in Atlanta, a much bigger and better-equipped facility. Eleven surgeries and one CAT scan later (a CAT scan was a relatively new procedure in 1978), the worrisome leak was found, and the blood loss was stopped. Shrapnel had nicked an artery about a half-inch from Flynt's heart, leaving a small but potentially deadly tear.

Stopping the blood loss was just the beginning of a very long road for Flynt. The bullet had damaged a bundle of nerves at the base of his spine; his legs were left paralyzed but in excruciating pain. If the slug had actually severed his spine, he would have still been left paralyzed, but free of the pain that he constantly endured, pain that in his words, felt like he was "suspended in a vat of boiling water."

Althea flew to Georgia to be by her husband's side as soon as she heard the news of the shooting. The day after the shooting, Cambria picked up comedian Dick Gregory, a friend of Flynt's, at the airport and drove him straight to the hospital to be with his friend. Gregory had recommended the fad diet that Flynt had been following and by doing so, he may well have contributed to his friend's survival. In fact, both Flynt and Reeves were fortunate enough to have nearly empty lower intestines when they were shot; the risk of infection was much lower as a result.

On the drive from the airport, Cambria recalls that Gregory ducked low in the passenger seat of the car as he rode with the attorney through the city of Atlanta. Rumors were spinning about the reason for the sniper attack in the heart of the South; considering the region's reputation for deep-rooted racism, Gregory, an African American, preferred to be safe rather than sorry. Al Goldstein, the abrasive publisher of *Screw* magazine, also flew to be at Flynt's side when he received news of the shooting. According to Cambria, Goldstein, who was Jewish, wore a bulletproof vest during the entire time he spent in Atlanta.

Reeves remained in Button Gwinnett Hospital for twenty-seven days, and the grand total of his medical bills at the end of that time was $18,000, which Flynt paid in full. Letters of support and encouragement came to him from all over the world, a phenomenon that for the rest of his life impressed him. When Gene Reeves's path crossed Larry Flynt's back in 1978, he had no way of knowing just how much of an impact that crossing would have. It brought him fame, it brought him infamy, and it very nearly cost him his life.

According to Reeves, many who were closely involved with the obscenity trial, the shooting, and the fallout were not aware that Flynt went above and beyond that first act of kindness toward his now former attorney, sending weekly checks to Reeves during his long but complete recovery. In the weeks and months that followed the shooting, Reeves gained a measure of spirituality and awareness that he'd never had before. Within a year of the ambush, he was divorced, just one of the decisions that came along with his new awareness.

In the end a few scars were all that remained on Reeves's body to tell the story of that horrible, beautiful spring day back in 1978. He was quick to add that his four-week stay in Button Gwinnett Hospital can be credited for his giving up a lethal three-pack-a-day smoking habit. "When it was time for me to go home and the nurse said I could have a cigarette, I didn't want one. And I've never touched them since," Reeves said.

The long-term result of Flynt's injuries, on the other hand, was painful and debilitating paralysis. The ambush-style shooting in Georgia, paired with the ruthless and unyielding pain that wracked his body for years afterward, had gutted his fledgling dedication to Christianity. He renounced both Jesus Christ and religion shortly after the incident, much to Ruth Carter-Stapleton's dismay.

For years, Flynt's doctors did the best they could to manage his searing pain with medication. So great was his agony that his doctors tried every tool at their disposal in the fight to alleviate it. Valium, Percodan, Percocet, Librium, Demerol, Morphine and Dilaudid, in the form of both pills and injections, became part of Flynt's daily life. More accurately, his daily life revolved around these heavy-weight painkillers, with the hours between doses crawling slowly by. Soon, the prescribed doses were not enough; he required more and more of the stuff just to get through the day. In almost no time, Larry Flynt, the once flamboyant, brilliant hustler, became a slave to the heavy-hitting medications, and so did his precious Althea. His sharp mind and driving passion became dulled and lethargic. Her husband's primary caregiver, Althea had sampled the doctors' lethal wares one time too many as she doled out relief to her husband. She once explained in an interview that using the drugs with her husband was the only way she could remain close to him during those dark years. Whatever the reasons, she too fell prey to the sly promise of escape whispered so convincingly by narcotics.

Shortly after the shooting, and once surgeons had Flynt stabilized and out of danger of dying from his injuries, he and Althea moved from Cincinnati to California. They purchased a sprawling mansion that had been built by Errol Flynn and previously occupied by the likes of Tony Curtis, Robert Stack, and Sonny and Cher. The dazed and injured couple retreated inside their mansion, sealed off their bedroom with a thick, custom-made, five-hundred-pound steel door, and then spent years behind that door secreted away from the world with only each other and their endless supply of powerful drugs by which to gauge reality. Althea spent a fortune procuring cocaine, marijuana, Quaaludes, sleeping pills, and anything else she could find to ease Larry's pain, as well as her own. The seeds of paranoia, planted by the shock of the shooting and death threats too numerous to count (Larry had been warned many times by his advisors to wear a bulletproof vest), were watered well and fertilized with potent stimulants, rich narcotics, and seclusion. Flynt became obsessed with first one, then another, theory about who shot him, who hired that shooter, and why they had done so.

For years, while he writhed and screamed in pain that some doctors called "imaginary," Flynt tried desperately to find a doctor who would perform a radical surgery, one that would involve completely severing his spine. He had read about the procedure and understood that it was the only way to stop the relentless burning pain that had tormented him for years. In 1983, a doctor told Flynt about a surgery, one in which surgeons could cauterize nerves in the spinal cord and thereby eliminate pain. The procedure was being performed at Duke University in North Carolina. Not long after hearing about the miracle surgery, the pale, drug-addicted paraplegic arrived at Duke University hospital, ready to undergo the life-changing procedure.

Larry Flynt underwent the first in a series of surgeries that would repair the damage to the cluster of nerves near the base of his spine. The .44 Marlin Franklin used to shoot him had done its job. The deadly bullet had chewed its way through his body and left quite a lot of damage in its wake. Nevertheless, the procedure was a success. A second surgery four years later, and a third in 1994, slowly eased the unbearable pain and eventually paved the way for Flynt to wash his hands of the dreadful addiction. Still, the paranoia had already taken strong root, and even as Flynt extricated himself from the firm grip of the drugs, the conspiracy theories grew and multiplied.

Althea sought treatment for her addiction from a private clinic, but Flynt insisted on going cold turkey, against his doctors' advice. As a result, he slipped into a depression so dark and deep that at one time, he had seriously considered suicide.

The year 1983 marked a turning point for the porn king, though. With much of his pain alleviated after the first surgery that year, the old Flynt was back, raunchier and every bit as shockingly offensive as the Larry Flynt the world knew before the shooting. Sales of *Hustler* magazine had been flagging and readership dropping since Flynt had professed his acceptance of Jesus Christ under Carter-Stapleton's watchful tutelage. During the years that he spent in a drug-induced fog, his wife (and co-publisher) took over the production of the magazine, aiming to make it as scandalous and profitable as it once was. Despite her own reliance on her husband's smorgasbord of prescription drugs, she was making headway. In an attempt to infuse some much-needed cash in to the magazine, Althea sold their prized red chinchilla-lined Rolls Royce, as well as the pink airplane they had bought from the Elvis Presley estate. The magazine was back on track, and the couple's bank accounts were once again fat and healthy.

Althea stayed by her husband's side until the day she died, but Flynt often said that he couldn't figure out why. His paralysis had left him unable to sexually satisfy his twenty-nine year old wife. The two talked about the matter openly and frankly; after their marriage, Flynt continued to have sex with other women, but even then, Althea remained faithful to her husband. Her one rule was that her husband was never allowed to kiss another woman. She knew that her husband could never be satisfied by just one woman, even if that woman was his young wife. She knew that and accepted it, going so far as to steer *Hustler* models his way every now and then. But kissing was an intimacy that was hers alone, and she made no bones about that reservation with her husband. Flynt shared that information with reporter Leo Janos in an August 1983 *PEOPLE* magazine article about his life after the shooting. "She found me kissing one of the *Hustler* models and damned near broke my ribs, punching and kicking," Flynt recalled. Even in their famously open marriage, Althea expected the boundaries she set to be respected.

After the shooting and ensuing paralysis, Althea would shrug and say, simply, that she didn't want any other man besides her husband. His inability to perform for her and with her in bed was not an issue. Her love and her loyalty, while puzzling to Flynt, were his motivation to clean himself up, get off the drugs, and get on with his life. Ironically, his love for her is also what drove him to file for divorce from Althea, when he urged her to quit taking the narcotics and she refused. She moved out of the mansion, but the pair only stayed apart for a few weeks before she moved back in. They couldn't stand being apart.

That same August 1983 article in *PEOPLE* Magazine quoted him as saying, "I have no zest for life anymore. I came out of this ordeal an atheist. I'd gladly die tomorrow, except I know it would make Althea desperately unhappy, but damned if I know why."

Unable to engage in what some might call his single most pleasurable practice (sex) ever again, Flynt turned his again formidable mind and dogged persistence to his next favorite pastimes: shock, and his First Amendment right to create and publish it. Back in the plush Beverly Hills offices of *Hustler* magazine once again, and in a gold-plated wheelchair no less, he announced that the magazine would soon feature a virgin being de-flowered for the first time, right there on the slick, shiny pages of *Hustler*. Larry Flynt may have been left unable to perform sexually as a result of the shooting in Georgia, but his mind was as sharp as ever once the drugs had been scrubbed from it. He was back in business, but he still had another matter to tend to.

He was convinced that conspiracy was afoot with respect to his shooting, and he intended to make sure the District Attorney in Gwinnett County uncovered it, dragged it out into the light of day, and prosecuted it. He had begun hearing rumblings on that topic in 1983, word that a radical racist named Joseph Paul Franklin had acted alone in the shooting, but he wasn't buying such a simple explanation.

In 1984, Flynt sent a letter to the District Attorney of Gwinnett County, Bryant Huff. In it, he wrote,

"Huff, you can rest assured that I am not crazy, but I'm mad as hell at you incompetent assholes. I have the murder weapon. Now what do you think of those apples?"

He went on to say that an attorney would be contacting the DA's office to find out who hired Joseph Franklin to shoot him, and how much he was paid. He then intimated that the shooting was an ordered hit, because there was a fear that he would put Ruth Carter-Stapleton on the stand during the obscenity trial to talk about "sexual healing."

Later in that same correspondence, and in other letters written to Huff, Flynt said that there was a conspiracy among several Georgia lawmakers to have him killed. This theory suggested that a man named Clark Williams had been paid $25,000 by some Georgia politicos, namely Congressman Larry McDonald, Congressman Newt Gingrich, Speaker of the House Tom Murphy, and Senator Culver Kidd, to shoot him. He added that the local police were in on the plot and the cover-up. There was mention made of Lester Maddox, as well, the governor of Georgia from 1967 to 1971. Maddox was elected to office largely on the grounds that he opposed integration, which was being legislated in Georgia and throughout the South against the will of the majority of voters. Flynt's letters to Huff with respect to this theory were rambling and often disjointed. No conspiracy was ever identified, and none of the politicians named was ever charged with any wrongdoing, at least not in the matter of the Flynt shooting.

Flynt also asserted at one time that the Moral Majority of the country was responsible for the attempt on his life. In 1979, Baptist minister Jerry Falwell founded the country's Moral Majority. Christian fundamentalists, in response to the cultural and political upheaval of the '60s and '70s, pushed back against the changes with the muscle of the Moral Majority, and Falwell, with this charismatic manner and savvy political activism, was the face of the movement. The Moral Majority opposed many of the changes that characterized the two volatile decades, including the civil rights movement, women's rights, and gay rights. Very quickly, the Moral Majority grew to several million members nationwide, and the organization's crowning achievement, in the opinion of some, was the 1980 election of Ronald Reagan to the US presidency.

In 1983, *Hustler* magazine printed a parody of Falwell, lobbing the assertion that the super-preacher lost his virginity to his own mother in a Lynchburg, Virginia, outhouse. Falwell and his followers were incensed by the piece, and the Reverend filed a lawsuit that was eventually heard by the United States Supreme Court. Falwell charged that the assertion that he had committed incest with his mother (in an outhouse, no less) had caused him both personal and professional angst. Flynt maintained that the piece was simple satire, protected by his First Amendment rights. Eventually, Flynt and *Hustler* were found to be perfectly within their rights by publishing the satirical claim. No connection was ever established between Falwell, The Moral Majority, and the attempt of Flynt's life.

Yet another of Flynt's speculations about who may have put a price on his head, and possibly his favorite theory, was that the CIA had tried to permanently silence the outspoken publisher. In

January 1978, just two months before the assault, *Hustler* magazine offered a one million dollar reward to anyone who could provide information proving an assassination conspiracy to kill John F. Kennedy. Flynt theorized that Lee Harvey Oswald was just one of four actual assassins, and he was intended to be the fall guy all along. The CIA was jumpy in those days, with the House Select Committee's investigations into the president's shooting in full swing. The idea of a CIA conspiracy designed to silence Flynt and his allegations, to many, did not seem very far-fetched. Why else would the Committee's findings be sealed for fifty years, until the year 2029? It wasn't just Flynt who smelled a rat.

By far the most outlandish theory Flynt suggested with respect to the shooting was that Billy Carter, the wayward and sometimes embarrassing brother of president Jimmy Carter, had hired someone to kill him. But this idea had at least one foot in plausible reality; in a January, 1978, taping of the Phil Donahue Show in Chicago, Billy Carter said (referring to Flynt), "He made some kind of wild comments about my mother, and I didn't like it. I got one man looking out for him. When he sees him, the first thing he's going to do is knock the hell out of him." Two months later, Flynt was gunned down in Georgia, Carter's home state. While the timing of the remarks and the shooting were suspect, no one, including police chief Crunkleton in Lawrenceville, took Carter seriously (not an uncommon reaction to Billy and his strange antics).

This theory resurfaced several years after the shooting, during an interview between Joseph Franklin and WAGA television news assignment editor, Karen Marshall, a friend of Det. Michael Cowart's. According to a July 17, 1984, interview between Marshall and Cowart, the newswoman said that Franklin had summoned her to visit him, saying that he had a "big scoop" for her. At the time, Franklin was incarcerated in the Hamilton County, Tennessee, jail. Marshall did go to Chattanooga to interview Franklin, and a week later, Cowart interviewed her. He was hoping that Franklin had given her specific information about the 1978 shooting in Gwinnett County. And indeed, he had.

Joseph Franklin told Karen Marshall that Billy Carter promised to pay him ten thousand dollars to shoot and kill Larry Flynt. Carter's reason for making this business deal, according to Franklin, was that Flynt had insulted his mother. Franklin said he was to receive five thousand dollars up front, and the other five thousand after he killed Flynt. He told Marshall that he never received the second five thousand dollars, since he failed to actually kill the bothersome pornographer.

When Marshall asked him how he knew Billy Carter, he said that he had been "cruising" through Americus, Georgia, and drove through Plains, Georgia, where the Carter family lived. He stopped at the gas station that president Carter's brother ran, and the two men started talking. "We had a lot in common. We're both rednecks," Franklin told Marshall. In an attempt to substantiate the tale he had spun for the reporter, Franklin added touches intended to lend credence to his story. He said he visited the Carters' family home. He said he told Billy that he didn't think that a man who ran a gas station could afford to pay anyone ten thousand dollars, but Billy said that he could get the money from his "Libyan buddies."

Cowart knew full well that Franklin was lying with this outlandish tale, but he also knew that, if Franklin had given Marshall factual details about the shooting that only the shooter would know, the interview tapes would be critical in building a legal case against him.

Cowart recalls what happened next, with pain and disappointment still tinting his words this many years later.

Citing station policy, Marshall refused to turn the tapes over to Cowart and the Gwinnett County PD. She said that they had been lost, even when Cowart politely but firmly told her that they could be subpoenaed if necessary. "We were friends. She could see how much that hurt me personally," Cowart recalls years later. "She then told me that Franklin had claimed that Billy Carter had hired him, but that was the extent of the information that she shared with me."

"I wasn't asking her to cross any ethical lines. But she used that old line that all reporters use—'It's against station policy. You'll have to talk to my boss.' That was one of those times I remember clearly, understanding that not all of us did what we did to find the truth. To some, it was all just a game."

The tapes from Marshall's Hamilton County interview with Franklin, to Cowart's knowledge, have never surfaced. To this day, the details of that forty-five-minute interview between Franklin and Marshall are known only to the two participants, and now one of them is dead.

CHAPTER 15
Up Is Down, and Down Is Up
(1984)

Detective Michael Cowart

THE DECEMBER 1983 phone conversation that I had with Joe left Bruno, Mac, and me with some heavy work to do. Because we were investigating a shooting that happened almost six years earlier, and because everybody and their brother tried to claim responsibility for it, we actually had to work to *disprove* Joe's confession in order to prove it to be true. I knew, as we all did, that Joseph Franklin shot Larry Flynt and Gene Reeves in cold blood, but knowing that and being able to prove it are two very different things. I learned quickly that Franklin was a master manipulator, and I'll give you an example of what I mean.

On July 29, 1977, just before 9:00 p.m., the Beth Sholom synagogue in Chattanooga, Hamilton County, Tennessee, was completely destroyed by an explosion. A bomb had been placed in the center of the building, in a crawl space underneath the floor. It had been detonated by an electrical extension cord that ran about two hundred feet from the synagogue to a nearby motel. There, it had been plugged into an electrical outlet to ignite the charge. Investigators noted the unmistakable odor of exploded dynamite when they arrived on the scene, a very telling sign that the explosion was no accident.

The Federal Bureau of Alcohol, Tobacco and Firearms investigated all available leads, and none of them panned out or even produced a person of interest. They closed the case in November 1979. In 1984, nearly five years later, the Chattanooga Police Department received information that Joseph Paul Franklin had made statements regarding the synagogue bombing; on February 29, 1984, on site at the US Penitentiary at Marion, Illinois, and in the presence of an ATF agent and a Chattanooga police officer, Franklin waived his Miranda rights, voluntarily confessing to the bombing and possession of explosives. He further stated that he had intended for the explosion to be timed with an evening service when the synagogue would have had people in it. Fortunately, that evening's service had ended early, and only the building was destroyed. There was no loss of life or injuries.

Interesting, no? At the same time he was talking to me about the Flynt shooting, Joe had reached out to another jurisdiction regarding another crime for which he was not even a suspect, and confessed to that crime. I'm sure that by now, you could have guessed what he wanted in exchange for sharing that information: a transfer out of Marion.

Well, the folks in Hamilton County, Tennessee, weren't about to have a confession to the bombing without pursuing prosecution. The Jewish community in Chattanooga, and the community as a whole really, had been shaken to the core by the sheer randomness and violence of the act. The trial took place from July 10 to 12, 1984. What the District Attorney thought would be an open-and-shut case and a slam-dunk for his department turned out to be anything but. Nothing with Franklin was ever open-and-shut; there were always surprises, twists, and turns.

The attorneys appointed to defend Joe in this matter were good ones, highly reputable. Their defense boiled down to this: Joseph Franklin would have confessed anything to anyone who would listen if he thought it would get him out of Marion. The course they chose to navigate was an unusual one; in order to prove their point in this matter, they stressed to the jury repeatedly that Joe actually did commit several heinous crimes, and he committed them because of his hatred of blacks and Jews, as well as his warped political ideas. They would reiterate to the jury that, not only had he been attacked by a group of black inmates and stabbed several times, but he was also kept in complete isolation except for his interaction with guards. He was a high escape risk, and he was at high risk of attack from the black population in the prison. Joe hated the isolation and the maximum security at Marion, and he wanted out, at any cost or risk. That was his defense, and it was a pretty smart one. He was lying, said his attorneys, just to be free of Marion.

To prove their point, Joe's defense team called me to Chattanooga to testify. In fact, I was the only witness they called. They intended to make the point that he had confessed to me that he shot Larry Flynt in Georgia, for the same reason he confessed to the bombing in Tennessee.

When I was called to the stand to testify as to what Joe told me during that December 1983 phone call, Joe's attorney asked me questions that would point to his dissatisfaction with his incarceration at Marion. They asked me whether Joe had complained to me about not being able to go outside, and I said that yes, he had. They asked me whether he had made up wild stories about his fear for his life, such as the Thevis conspiracy, and I said that yes, he had. They asked me whether I was aware that Joe had been attacked by several black inmates, stabbed, then sodomized with a steel bar, and that was when all hell broke loose in what was to have been an open-and-shut case.

When Joe heard his attorney assert that the attack on him included a sexual assault, he jumped up out of the Defendant's chair and began yelling, "You're fired!" He followed that declaration with vehement denials of any such sexual attack, or even an attempt at one. The defense attorney withdrew the question, and at that point, Franklin took over his own defense. I was excused as a witness.

On the following day, when closing arguments were to be made, Franklin insisted that he be allowed to make his closing argument to the jury himself. The judge allowed him to proceed, but not before advising the jury that his remarks were not to be taken as statements of fact; rather, he was allowed to state a defense position just as any defense attorney would.

Joe then began his bizarre, meandering statement, telling the jury that his remarks were unrehearsed and that he had "just an hour ago" decided to present his own closing argument. After making a terse comment regarding the stabbing incident at Marion, he stated to the jury, "I want to make your job a little easier here, as far as your deliberations go. You know, I admit to you, I bombed the synagogue. You know I did it. You know, and I'll tell it to anybody around. It was a synagogue of Satan." He continued, explaining why he bombed the synagogue, basing his position on his interpretation of the Bible. He specifically referenced the Book of Revelations, that mysterious final book of the Bible that tells of the second coming of Christ, fire, sorrow, horsemen, death, and eternal damnation. He elaborated on the Jewish conspiracy in which he believed wholeheartedly, claiming that "(Jews) control the American Government. They control the news media. They control all different branches of the US Government. The communist nations are all controlled by Jews, and all the western democracies are controlled by Jews." He delved deeper into his beliefs, explaining that the "Kahzar Jews are trying to destroy the white race through race mixing and communism."

It was becoming evident, to me and I assume to others in the courtroom, that Joe took this opportunity to not only spread his theory of a Jewish conspiracy (always justifying his acts, remember), but also to urge jurors and anyone else within earshot to act. "For everybody to—the only way that the white race can be saved now and get out of the trouble that they're in today, is for everybody to fast and get on their knees and praise the Lord. And I just hope that everybody here does that and accepts Jesus Christ as their personal savior." When he stopped speaking, he nervously straightened his glasses and looked away from the jurors, a habit that had been years in the making. When Joe Franklin was on his soapbox about his politics of hatred, he was bold and confident. Otherwise, he was self-conscious about his disability and appearance.

When he concluded his speech and sat down, one of his defense attorneys (both gentlemen remained Joe's counsel in spite of his unceremonious "firing" the day before) rose to deliver his closing arguments. Basically, he told jurors that this was a very unusual case, one in which defense attorneys were asking jurors not to believe their client and in which the prosecutor was asking them to believe him.

I share this account, which is one of many to be sure, in an attempt to illustrate the upside-down, carnival-like atmosphere that Joe Franklin and his beliefs carried to every situation, every conversation, every interaction. He was an enigma, the black side of human consciousness, an apparition from which people turned in disgust but that secretly fascinated those same people. The very words that he spoke were no doubt on the minds of many Americans, especially southern Americans, who had survived the turmoil of the '60s and '70s and lived to tell about it. Of course, very few of those people thought along the same extreme lines as Franklin; their hatred and mistrust were watered down, murky, and not as well defined as his. Their dissatisfaction had done little more than dull their zest for life and sharpen their hate of blacks. I do believe that Joseph Franklin was the product of a horribly abusive childhood, yes, but if I am to be honest, he was also the product of a South in the throes of change, unwelcome change to many. He was our distorted reflection in the funhouse mirror, and on close inspection, he was terrifying.

Convicted by the Chattanooga jury, Joe was sentenced to fifteen to twenty-one years for the bombing, and six to ten years for possession of explosives, to be served consecutively. Of course, he would have to complete his time at Marion before he'd have the pleasure of satisfying the people of Chattanooga. His dance card was getting full. In the end, his attempt to manipulate the media and the justice system had not achieved the results he desired. There he still sat, rotting in a prison that he hated.

On July 12, 1984, the last day of the bombing trial in Chattanooga, Joe waived his right to have his trial attorneys Jerry Summers and Hugh Moore, Jr., present as he again spoke with me about the facts surrounding the March 6, 1978, shooting of Larry Flynt. Of course, his counsel advised him strongly against talking with me about that matter at all, much less without their presence, but he would not be swayed. He was determined to keep fishing for a prison transfer, and he would talk to anyone who could help toward that end. Now, we were his best bet.

CHAPTER 16
The Stumble
(1980)

GOD IT'S HOT. The sun hammered down on Joe Franklin's back and neck without mercy; twice already he had chugged from the already-warm bottle of water he had stashed in his car, and twice, the water had threatened to come right back up. Sweat rolled into his eyes like salty raindrops. July in Tennessee was always hotter than hell, and the humidity that went along with it made the air unbearably thick and difficult to breathe. His shirt was sticking to his back in large wet patches; still, he could feel more sweat rolling down his back and underneath the waist of his jeans, soaking his shorts. He had known, as he always did, that if he stayed hidden there in the grass long enough, a suitable target would wander into his sights. Sure enough there were two of them in there right now, stuffing pizza in their mouths, talking and laughing, probably kissing and making the other patrons sick to their stomachs. Neither of them had any idea that their lives were about to come to a screeching halt, or that their last meal would be a double-pepperoni thick crust pizza, with extra cheese. Well, that was true for one of them, anyway.

This is getting too easy, like taking candy from a baby. A drop of sweat rolled into Franklin's good eye, and he winced at the sting of it. He wiped the sweat from his brow with the palm of his hand, leaving a dirty black swipe across his thin face as he did so. He adjusted his glasses, more out of habit than necessity; the lenses were grimy and smeared with sweat. He had been crouched out here for about an hour, behind this pile of rocks and some thick patches of high grass, about 100 yards behind a Chattanooga Pizza Hut. His car was parked just a few yards away, beyond that rise, pointed toward the highway and ready to go as soon as he accomplished his mission. He was lucky today, if that's how you wanted to look at it; he didn't have to wait all that long to spot a race mixing couple. In fact, it was getting to be more and more common to see them out in public, flaunting their sin for all the world to see and not giving a damn what people thought about it. Well, it made him furious. Today, they'd give a damn all right. Today they'd be sorry they had ever broken God's law by lying with somebody not of their own race. *Yes, these two will make fine examples of what happens when niggers and white folks mix.*

He was waiting for his prey to come out of the restaurant. He had seen them go in, so he knew they had to come out at some point. He also knew where they had parked; he had chosen this spot not only for the cover it provided him, but it also gave him the perfect angle for two sure kill shots. *Come on out, you two. Come and get you some of this. I'll show you how God deals with race mixers.*

It had been about four months since he had slid on out of Gwinnett County, right under the noses of the cops down there. Four months since he made the phone call about Jesus taking care of business. Four months since he had disassembled the Marlin, sawed the barrel into three or four pieces, and thrown the wood stock in a dumpster. He had decided to hunt again today, having laid low for a while after that mess down in Georgia. The cops down there, even the FBI, were running around like chickens with their heads cut off, with no more of an idea today who had shot Larry Flynt than they had back in March. He was certain that his name had never come up in any of the discussions among law enforcement agencies. He could draw them a map and write out a full confession, and they still couldn't find their asses with both hands and a flashlight. He almost felt sorry for them. If half of what he'd been reading in the newspapers was true, there were some pretty wild theories floating around out there about who shot Flynt and why. They were comical, really.

He had work to do, though. He had stayed out of commission long enough. His dedication to the cause of inciting a race war, of bringing hell's fury down on the heads of those who weren't of the pure race, had not flagged one bit. If anything, it had grown stronger.

The side entry door to the Pizza Hut opened, and out walked Bryant Tatum and his girlfriend Nancy Hilton. Tatum was a black man; Nancy, white. It was a disgrace. Tatum exited the restaurant first, then held the door for his girlfriend, smiling at her and taking her arm. *There you are. Smile for the camera, you race mixing asshole. It'll be the last time, I promise you that.* The couple walked arm in arm along the sidewalk and stepped out onto the blacktop, holding hands, laughing, not the least bit ashamed. Joe's face burned and his vision blurred, and this time it had nothing to do with the blistering Tennessee heat. Just seeing them together like that, so openly unashamed, made him sick.

Without the cover of the thick, dry grass and piles of rock in which he was hiding, he would have been exposed for the couple and all of Chattanooga to see. As it was, though, they had no idea that a killer was watching them, and the fact that they were together made him hate them so much that he would kill them in cold blood. They had no idea that in a matter of minutes, their lives would be changed forever.

Joe was squatting in the tall grass, his weapon leaning against a hefty gray chunk of concrete, waiting patiently to be summoned to duty. Now, it was time. With practiced, quick smoothness, Franklin reached down and snatched up a 12-gauge shotgun, the perfect tool for today's business. You could shoot a 12-gauge with pretty impressive accuracy from a distance, and still do a hell of a lot of damage. He called the 12-gauge his "statement maker."

With the stock settled back into his shoulder, he leveled the gun and got a bead on the man as he ambled to his car. *The pain. Damn.* He squeezed his eyes shut and tried in vain to will it away. His head was pounding, the throb and the insistence of it nearly blinding him. The headaches were getting worse, so bad that he often vomited from the deafening sound and the pounding ache. It wasn't just the heat that was beating the sickening drum today, though. It was pure, undiluted hate.

In another quick and practiced motion, he leaned the shotgun away from his body and puked into the dry dirt and grass that hid him from view. Everything he had eaten since yesterday, it seemed, ended up there at his feet in a sick, steaming pile. He sat there, looking down at his own vomit, tears and sweat dripping from his face and mixing with the mess at his feet. Retching and heaving a time or two more, he decided that he had nothing left to give and went back to his work. The headache backed off a bit but refused to leave. He directed his attention back to the targets and the work at hand.

The man's body shielded his girlfriend's from Franklin's sight completely. *He's a big one. I'll probably get extra credit for bagging him.* She was next. Nancy giggled at something her man had just said, and she stood on tiptoe to kiss him on the mouth. Franklin felt his stomach roll at the sight. The anger inside him was building, and he focused his energy on pushing it back down deep, where it lived and roiled inside him. Emotion had no place in his business today. Emotion could lead to mistakes, and mistakes were not acceptable.

Joe followed the big man's slow gait with the tip of the shotgun, the barrel aimed at dead center mass. Without hesitation, he cocked the hammer and pulled the trigger. The shotgun kicked, nearly knocking him backward into the tall, chigger-infested grass. The bullet must have traveled a hell of a lot faster than the sound of the shot, because by the time other customers in the parking lot heard the blast, Tatum was already down, a warm, red patch spreading on the front of his new white shirt. He had bought it just last night, for this date with Nancy. In a state of shock, the man looked down at his new shirt, wondering what that stain was. *My new shirt. It's ruined.*

The woman stopped short on the striped blacktop. Gone was the sick-sweet expression she had on her face just a moment ago. It had been replaced with a look of shock and disbelief. It said, "What the hell? What just happened?" The look said that she knew she was witnessing something terrifying, but her mind couldn't yet put a name to it. He enjoyed the scene for a second or two longer, then took deadly aim at her. Now she was screaming in panic, fear taking over. Staring wide-eyed at her lover crumpled on the hot pavement at her feet, she looked behind her, then up the hill, directly at the spot where Joe was hiding. If not for the grass and large rocks, she would have been looking right at him. "Bryant? Oh my God, Bryant!" She was sobbing and screaming at the same time. *Disgusting. How 'bout I shut you up, whore? I've heard just about enough.*

He jacked the hammer and pulled the trigger again, just as Nancy dropped to her knees beside her dying lover. Her face was inches from his, and she slipped her hand under his head, cradling it. The customary crowd had begun to gather, most of them according to their usual sheep-like behavior—keeping a safe distance but gawking just the same. It was like a movie script.

Bryant Tatum's eyes stared straight through Nancy's, to something well beyond hers. She had no way of knowing that he was gone before he even hit the ground.

That one movement, dropping to her knees beside her dying lover, saved Nancy Hilton's life. The shotgun blasted a second time, the bullet aimed dead center of the panicked woman's chest. Instead, since she dropped to the ground to cradle her lover, it struck her in the shoulder, chewing away some flesh but not taking her life.

She screamed again, fully in the grip of the panic now. She was hysterical. *Shut the fuck up*, he thought, stumbling to his feet and staggering to his parked car. If he had the time to spare, he would have taken another shot at her. Instead, he stopped to puke again. Nothing came up, but he tried just the same.

He turned and surveyed his handiwork one more time, watching the crowd gather and the onlookers scramble back and forth like ants under a magnifying glass. He could just now hear the sirens. It would be minutes before they arrived on the scene and began trying to figure out what the hell had just happened.

Franklin turned, took a couple of steps, and ducked inside his car. Throwing the 12-gauge onto the back seat, he turned the key in the ignition and slowly drove away from the scene, taking off down I-24 for parts unknown. He knew he had hit them both, and he knew that the man was dead; if not, he soon would be. No one could take a hit like that in the stomach and lose that much blood and live to tell about it. The bitch was another story. She moved after he had her in his sights; when he pulled the trigger the second time, she had taken the bullet in her shoulder as best he could tell. When he read the newspaper account of the shooting the next day, he wasn't surprised to learn that the woman had, in fact, survived the attack. *Damn.* Still, his list of successful assaults on targets was growing. Surely there were people out there who were paying attention, who were getting the message. Surely, someday soon, the uprising of decent, white, God-fearing citizens would begin. He was sending a clear message. Was anyone listening?

On October 8, 1977, about five months before the shooting in Gwinnett County, Franklin shot and killed Gerald Gordon as he left a bar mitzvah at the Brith Sholom Kneseth Israel Congregation in suburban St. Louis, Missouri. Joe had just robbed a bank in Arkansas and bought a rifle from a private owner. Having selected that particular synagogue (any one would have done, really, as Jews everywhere were enemies of the white race), he had staked out the synagogue the day before the shooting, even driving ten-inch nails into a telephone pole about 100 yards away to serve as a rest for his rifle. He carried the 30.06 to the ambush location in a guitar case, and after the shooting, he abandoned the case in some bushes. A few days after the synagogue shooting, he ground the serial number off of the rifle and from then on handled it only while wearing gloves.

Gordon's wife and children watched in horror as he lay on the pavement in the synagogue parking lot, shaking and in shock, his life's blood pooling around him as he bled to death there on the pavement. He had been hit several times and stood no chance of surviving. Steven Goldman and William Ash, who were also leaving the synagogue, were wounded. As the chaos built to a fever pitch at Brith Sholom Kneseth Israel Congregation that afternoon, Joe Franklin hopped onto a bicycle that he had brought along for his escape, and pedaled to where he had parked his car. No one saw or heard the deadly sniper as he slipped silently away.

The only thing Franklin knew about Gerald Gordon, the only motive for shooting him like a rabid animal, was that Gordon was Jewish. He assumed that, because Gordon and his family had exited the synagogue just seconds before he was killed. The Missouri attack, a seemingly random sniper-style shooting, would ultimately be the one for which Franklin would be tried, convicted, and sentenced. It would be the killing for which he would ultimately give his own life in exchange, courtesy of the state of Missouri and its no-nonsense justice system. In 1997, Franklin would be tried and sentenced to death for the murder of Gerald Gordon. That was twenty years from now, though. As he crouched in the tall grass behind the Missouri synagogue and watched the panic spread, he had no way of knowing what the ultimate outcome would be; he just knew that he was doing his country and his race a service. In those precious few seconds immediately following the shooting of the Jewish husband and father, Joe Franklin simply relished the aftermath for as long as he could. When the sirens began to wail and shriek, that was his signal to leave.

After shooting Flynt and Reeves down in Georgia, Joseph Franklin went on a killing spree that spread from Utah to Tennessee, and it included almost every place in between. But the Gwinnett County shooting was not the first well-planned taste of blood that he enjoyed, not by far.

It's been said that, once a man has killed for sport or revenge, his thirst for killing is never quenched. In fact, it grows and in some men, it consumes them. Joe Franklin was consumed, both with killing and with his reason for killing, his "mission." In his lifetime, he intended to see a race war ignited. He intended to be the one who touched the fire to the torch that would someday lead the way. And he would do it one murder at a time, if that's what it took to shake white men awake, to stir them to take up arms and take back the country, which was rightfully theirs anyway.

Shootings were more satisfying to Franklin than were bombings. Shootings were up close and personal. Bombings had the potential to take out more targets, but they were messy. He liked to see his targets, and he loved to see the searing damage that a bullet did as it tore into them. If he was really lucky, he'd get to see the expressions on their faces, their blood pumping out onto the ground underneath them. He always ambushed his targets from a distance, so they had to spin around in just the right direction for him to get a glimpse of their faces as they died. It was a real treat for him when they did.

Bombings, on the other hand, were not nearly as satisfying, but they got a lot of attention. Bombings made the news, and not just in the local coverage area. They usually made national news. His first bombing was a pitifully impotent attempt in Rockland, Maryland, back in July 1977. The target was Jewish lobbyist Morris Amitay's home and family. Franklin constructed the bomb himself, and when Amitay and his family were away one evening, he placed it underneath the house, in a crawlspace. He had made some miscalculations, however, in the building of the bomb as well as in determining its placement under the house. As a result, he succeeded only in blowing up the Amitays' kitchen.

Neither Amitay nor his family were harmed in the incident, but the explosion killed the family dog. Later, Franklin would joke with Cowart about the bombing, laughing about "blowing up a kosher dog."

Four days after the Amitay bombing, he bombed the Beth Sholom Synagogue in Chattanooga. He was convicted of that bombing in July, 1984, and was sentenced to thirty-one years in prison. Tennessee would have to wait its turn, though. He was booked up for quite a while by now.

On August 7, 1977, Joe turned up in Madison, Wisconsin. He robbed a bank that same day and later, he shot and killed Alphonse Manning, Jr., and his white female companion, Toni Schwenn. They were simply walking together in a parking lot, and they probably never knew what hit them. The shots were clean and mortal. Franklin just happened to be in the "right place at the right time," saw the interracial couple, and murdered them on the spot.

He represented himself in that matter, and when Judge William D. Byrne asked him at the conclusion of the February 1986 trial whether he had any comments, Franklin replied, "No, your honor." According to a February 15, 1986 article in the *New York Times,* the jury deliberated for just two hours, and the judge immediately sentenced Franklin to two consecutive life terms, saying, "The defendant's history of violence, terror and murder prompts this court to do all it can so that he will never kill again."

In October of 1977, Franklin opened fire on a crowd gathered outside Brith Sholom Kneseth Israel congregation in Richmond Heights, Missouri, the incident in which he killed Gerald Gordon. In 1997, he was tried and convicted for murdering Gordon, and he received the death sentence in Missouri.

On February 2, 1978, Joe Franklin shot and killed Johnny Brookshire, a black man, and his white wife, Joy Williams, in

Atlanta. The couple were just twenty-two and twenty-three years old.

About a month later, he shot Larry Flynt and Gene Reeves in Lawrenceville, Georgia. A few months after that shooting and his narrow escape, Franklin ambushed Bryant Tatum and Nancy White outside the Chattanooga Pizza Hut.

On July 12, 1979, in Doraville, Georgia, Taco Bell manager Harold McIver was shot as he stood in front of the restaurant's plate glass window. The blast came from 150 yards away; he never even saw the shooter. As soon as Franklin saw the window shatter and McIver fall at a haphazard angle across the booth he was cleaning, he ducked back into his car and drove calmly away, so as not to draw attention to himself. Later, Franklin shared with a fellow inmate that he shot McIver, a black man, because "he associated with a lot of white women."

Five weeks later, in Falls Church, Virginia, Franklin shot twenty-eight-year-old William Taylor, another black man. Two months after that, he fatally shot interracial couple Jesse Taylor and Marion Bresette.

On December 5, 1979, he murdered fifteen-year-old prostitute Mercedes Lynn Masters, after having sex with her and subsequently learning that she also had had sex with black men. A few weeks later, he shot and killed Lawrence Reese, a black man living in Indianapolis. Two days after that, he killed Leo Thomas in the same city.

On May 2, 1980, in Wisconsin, Franklin fatally shot Rebecca Bergstrom, a white woman.

On May 29, 1980, Civil Rights Leader and Urban League President Vernon Jordan, Jr., accompanied by Martha Coleman, left the Marriott Hotel in Fort Wayne, Indiana. He didn't know it, but a cold-blooded serial killer had been stalking him for two days, waiting for this very moment.

A couple more steps. Let me get a good look at you. As Jordan approached his car, Franklin opened fire, wounding the man seriously. His female companion was not injured. Then-president Jimmy Carter visited Jordan in the hospital following the attack, and coverage of that visit was news network CNN's first story ever aired. Years later, Franklin would be tried for Jordan's shooting and acquitted of the crime. He later confessed to the shooting, many times, when talking to fellow inmates, the press, lawyers, and even to cops. Not everyone believed him, whether he denied or confessed to the shooting. It was hard for people to believe that he could get away with such a crime, especially in light of the rising popularity of civil rights activists. It was also hard for people to believe that he would be reckless enough to brag about the shooting to the very people who could charge him with the crime.

On June 8, 1980, Franklin shot and killed two young black boys, cousins Darrell Lane, fourteen, and thirteen-year-old Dante Evans Brown. Hot, irritated, and impatient, he had been hiding and waiting on a Cincinnati overpass until ten o'clock that night, hoping to see an interracial couple walk into his line of sight. If he did (and he was sure that he would), he had a .44 Ruger by his side to take care of the situation. After an hour or so of waiting, his patience was growing thin. When he saw the two young cousins walking along the street down below, his mood lifted. *Well, at least I won't go home empty-handed. I can still get me two today.*

Years later, he confessed to killing the two boys and was given two life sentences as a result. In a 2013 death row interview with journalist Beth Karas, Franklin said that he was deeply sorry about killing the two children.

Recalling the shootings from a telephone interview booth in the Missouri prison, Franklin recalls the incident with uncanny clarity. "I remember I shot the biggest one first. When I did, the other one bolted and ran. I couldn't get him in the crosshairs because he was moving too fast, so I just swung my gun left in the direction he was running, and shot. When I read about it in the newspaper the next day, I couldn't believe that I killed them both. I thought (the newspapers) were lying." When asked whether he truly regretted shooting the young cousins, he answered, "I realize now that it was wrong to shoot those boys. I just kept hearing about teenage black boys raping white women when I lived in DC, and I thought it was an outrage. Back then, I guess I thought that they were all like that. I see now that that way of thinking was wrong. Am I a racist today? No."

In Johnstown, Pennsylvania, Franklin fatally shot Arthur Smothers and Kathleen Mikula, an interracial couple, on June 15, 1980.

On June 25, 1980, Nancy Santomero and Vicki Durian were hitchhiking along a Pocahontas County, West Virginia, road. Joseph Paul Franklin was driving along that same road, and when he saw the two young women, he stopped and picked them up. The three conversed as they traveled down the two-lane highway, and then one of them (he never could remember which, even when he voluntarily confessed to the crime to an Ohio assistant prosecutor years later) told him that she had an African-American boyfriend. Without saying another word, Franklin pulled his car off onto the shoulder of the road and reached under his seat for a pistol. Demanding that both of the women get out of his car, Franklin shot them where they stood on the side of the road. Just like that, in plain sight in the middle of the day. Of course, the road was deserted, but someone could have come along at any moment and seen him murder those two women. Some law enforcement officers believe that by this point in his life, and after having killed so many people, Franklin believed he was invincible.

In yet another irony (ironies seemed to swirl around Franklin like honeybees), a Florida man named Jacob Beard had been convicted in 1993 of shooting the same two women and was serving time in a federal prison as a result. When Franklin eventually confessed, Beard was freed and granted a new trial.

By this time, the FBI was watching Joseph Franklin with keen interest, as his crimes had escalated from an occasional event to what one investigator called a "frenzy" once all the puzzle pieces had been fitted properly into place. While the agency didn't share much information with other law enforcement entities, the Gwinnett County District Attorney and police officers had begun to hear rumblings of some sort of connection between the racist from Alabama, and the seemingly unrelated murders sprinkled throughout the eastern to midwestern United States over a three-year period.

In August 1980, Joe Franklin traveled to Salt Lake City, Utah. Investigators and reporters wondered and hypothesized for years as to why a racist serial killer would include Utah in his hunting grounds, but Franklin himself answered the question in a 2013 death row interview he granted to reporter Brooke Adams of the *Salt Lake City Tribune*. He had been baptized into the Church of the Latter Day Saints in 1974 when he lived in Atlanta, and in 1975, he simply decided that he wanted to see the hometown of his new faith. He liked the stance that the church took on fornication, and he liked the fact that the consumption of alcohol, tea, tobacco, and coffee were frowned upon. They were all either stimulants or depressants and as such, they were forbidden. During that first and subsequent trips to Utah, however, he did not like the rest of what he saw.

"I couldn't help but notice all the miscegenation going on there," he told Adams on the telephone. Inbreeding. Race mixing. In God's country. In the coming years, he didn't much like the changes he saw happening in the church, either. In 1978, the LDS Church allowed African Americans to become members of its lay priesthood. With that decision, Franklin was not only finished with Mormonism, but on an even greater scale, he had Salt Lake City, Utah, squarely in his crosshairs. What was going on there was wrong.

For all of his ghost-like habits and abilities, Joe Franklin's hatred of blacks often betrayed his otherwise under-the-radar presence. Most of the last three years of his life before his final arrest (he liked to compare his three-year crusade with the three years that preceded Christ's crucifixion) were spent on the road.

He lived and slept in seedy, low-rent motels. He ate in greasy-spoon diners. Even so, he had two simple standards that were non-negotiable. First, he would not sleep in a bed in which a black person had previously slept. Second, he would not eat in a restaurant in which a black person either cooked or served the food. He had no qualms about making those simple standards known, either.

It was a clerk in a Salt Lake City motel, in fact, who originally tipped off the police to Franklin's bizarre behavior and false registration information. In August 1980, Franklin arrived in Utah and booked a room in an inexpensive motel. His comments to the clerk were peculiar, to say the least.

"I'll take a room for the night, but I want you to be sure and look and see if any niggers have stayed in there first. I ain't staying in no room where a nigger's been." The clerk just stared at the man, his mouth hanging open in shock and disbelief. He had never heard anyone talk like that before. He wasn't sure how to respond.

"OK sir. Here you go, if you'll just sign the register. Name and license plate number please."

"Did you hear what I said? I ain't kidding."

"Yes, sir," was all the clerk could muster.

Franklin signed his name "James A. Cooper" and provided a false license plate number when he signed the motel registry. The clerk, who had listened in stunned silence to Franklin's odd demands about his room and the motel diner, waited for the odd guest to leave the lobby. His gut told him that the man who had just registered to stay a few nights in the motel was trouble, and trouble was the last thing he needed. Not on his shift, anyway. He walked out into the rainy Utah night, wrote down the actual license plate number on Franklin's car, then returned to the lobby to compare the tag numbers. Sure enough, the strange man had lied on the registry. The clerk wondered if he had even been honest about his name, though he had produced a driver's license with the name "James A. Cooper" on it. It wouldn't be the first time that he had been shown a fake driver's license, and he figured that one was about as fake as any he'd ever seen. Not wanting any trouble, he called the cops.

A man only hides like this man was doing for two reasons. He's either trying to hide from a woman or trying to hide from the law. From the looks of him, the clerk thought, women weren't much of an issue for this cat. He was sort of smallish for a man, his hair was thinning, and there was something wrong with his eyes. It was hard to tell with the glasses he wore, but one of them didn't look right. No, the clerk doubted that James A. Cooper was a womanizer. If he was running from the law (and that made more sense than the other possibility), he didn't want any part of it. This was a strange guy, and who knew what he was capable of? His cold behavior and outspokenness when it came to his hatred for blacks and Jews made Joe Franklin a memorable man. Motel clerks remembered him. Prostitutes remembered him. Pastors, neighbors, and waitresses remembered him. Once investigators were seriously looking at Joe for the string of murders and bank robberies, it was surprisingly easy to piece together his movements. He had left a trail of dumbfounded people in his wake. That turned out to be one of his few mistakes.

The Utah motel clerk called the police and reported the misinformation provided by Joe Franklin. An arrest warrant was issued for him, for stealing a car and providing false information to an innkeeper. He had been gone for a few days, however, by the time the cops bothered to show up and talk to him.

On August 20 of that same year, twenty-year-old Ted Fields and eighteen-year-old David Martin were shot and killed near Liberty Park in Salt Lake City, Utah. They were black men, and they had been jogging with two white women. Franklin had hunkered down behind a hill in a vacant field, hidden by grass and a small berm, and clutching a high-powered rifle. Crouching low in a hiding place just outside the park's boundaries, he settled in and waited. He knew that, if he waited long enough, he would make a kill that day. All he had to do was spot a black, a Jew, or a mixed-race couple. These days, he didn't have to wait very long before one of those crossed his path. When the joggers came in to view, he smiled. *Must be my lucky day. I can get me two of 'em.* And he did. That shooting, many locals said later, was the end of the innocence for the residents of Salt Lake City. If such a senseless, cold-blooded crime could take place in their idyllic community, many of its inhabitants Mormons, it could happen anywhere.

August 1980 also marked a rare stumble for Franklin during his three-year killing spree. He had no way of knowing that local police were looking for him because of his slip-up with the motel clerk. That Utah arrest warrant, along with the FBI's recent interest in him as a possible serial killer and bank robber, made Joe Franklin a wanted man. He was no longer a ghost. He was both visible and vulnerable. In fact, now he was being hunted, and he didn't even know it. Not yet, anyway.

Just after shooting the two young men near Liberty Park, he got into his car and immediately headed out west, first to Las Vegas and then to San Francisco. He stayed west of the Rockies for about two weeks and in September, he decided to head back east. In doing so, he passed through Florence, Kentucky.

Maybe he was mentally fatigued. Perhaps he had grown just a bit too cocky for his own good. Whatever the reason, he parked his car on the street in front of a hole-in-the-wall Florence diner when he went inside to eat, leaving a rifle in plain view on the back seat. As luck would have it, an observant police officer saw the firearm on the back seat when he, too, stopped at the diner for a cup of coffee, and perhaps a bite to eat. Checking the car's registration, the officer discovered that the license plate on the car was linked to an arrest warrant for car theft. When Franklin returned to his car after eating dinner, the alert officer arrested him, and he was detained in the Florence jail for questioning by both the Florence police and the FBI. A quick check on the drifter and car thief turned up an FBI alert and all of a sudden, Joseph Franklin was a very popular man. Seemed like everybody wanted to have a talk with the guy.

Franklin's drifter lifestyle, combined with his willingness to travel hundreds of miles in any direction following his commission of seemingly random crimes, had for years kept him off the radar of state and federal law enforcement. Oh the cops and feds knew about him all right, or at least they thought they did. For a long time, as far as they were concerned, Franklin was simply a radical racist, a petty criminal with minor charges to his name, but nothing more. The shooting in Salt Lake City changed all that, though. A prostitute he had been with at a motel there saw his photo flashed on a news report and immediately, she remembered the man with the wayward gaze and a burning hatred for blacks. He claimed to be a member of the Ku Klux Klan, railing and ranting about the way blacks were taking over the country, and about the white man's clear superiority to the darker race. After the two had finished having sex (a brief, bordering on violent, encounter), Joe asked the hooker for a list of all the black pimps in the area, as he planned to return and kill them (*Tuscaloosa News,* Oct, 29, 1980). The prostitute called the Salt Lake City police department when she saw the news story, and her call put both local and federal law enforcement hot on Joe's trail.

The FBI possessed some telling information about Franklin also, which as a matter of bureau policy they began sharing (grudgingly, some said) with other agencies in the early 1980s. On the face of it, the information didn't amount to much, really. Joe Franklin had several distinctive racist tattoos on his body, he had an affinity for firearms, and he often resorted to donating blood at blood banks in order to pocket some quick cash. In the end, that was all the information anybody needed.

CHAPTER 17
Making Good on a Promise
(1983–1984)

Detective Michael Cowart

The first thing I did when I got back to Gwinnett from the visit to Marion was contact the FBI-Atlanta Field Office and make arrangements to get the box of candy to them. They in turn would forward the candy to the FBI lab in Washington, DC, for analysis.

To my dismay (but not to my surprise), two months later I still had not received their report. Determined to remain true to my word, however, I wrote a letter to Franklin anyway, just to let him know where we stood on the matter.

November 25, 1983

"Dear Joe:

Sorry for the delay in writing, but I have been waiting to hear the results of the check we are making. As of this morning, I have not heard a report . . ." This was how I began my letter to him. In that letter, I also asked whether he had begun receiving the *Gwinnett Daily News* yet, as he had asked for it, and I had promised to try to get it delivered directly to him at Marion. "It's not the *New York Times*," I joked, "but they do keep pretty on top of things here." I also reminded him that I could not make any promises about getting him a lawyer, and that neither I nor the state of Georgia could do anything at all about getting him transferred out of a federal prison.

When we met with him in the prison at Marion, he asked us several times to see what we could do about getting him an attorney sent up from Georgia. While we discussed that possibility and the obvious obstacles we faced with it, I'll never forget his casual, almost glib, response. In fact, I believe that he was actually trying to make a joke when he said, "Just tell 'em not to send me Gene Reeves up here, you know what I'm talking about?" He laughed, then added, "Yeah, he happened to be in the wrong place at the wrong time, but uh, pretty unlucky dude, you know?" He laughed again, and since it was my job to earn his confidence and give him the impression that we were getting to be great friends, God help me, I laughed along with him. In doing the sort of work that I did, which included talking with the most evil man I had ever encountered, there were times that I had to step outside myself. I had to watch myself perform (literally, in the case of Joe Franklin) my job from a distance. Otherwise, I really think that after a while, I might have gone mad.

At any rate, Joe knew full well that we could not provide an attorney to represent him under any circumstances. He probably knew the legal reasons for that better than most attorneys would have known, and that was why he kept hounding us to relay his information, and various confessions, to the FBI. He was residing in a federal prison for the rest of his natural life (or so he thought at the time), and he was confessing to a list of felonies a mile long just to try to get some face time with an FBI agent. Still, the agency refused to give him the time of day. It was a real sticking point for Joe. I think it insulted him.

In my letter to him, I went on to share an anecdote about an inmate in the local correctional institute who had managed to steal and smuggle out a twenty-seven-lb. bag of marijuana. I confided to

Franklin that it would be a while before all the egg would be wiped off the department's face after that embarrassment. In closing, I thanked him for some newspaper clippings he had sent me, which were about various topics, mostly white supremacy and politics, but some about religion, too.

Sharing that anecdote about the marijuana (which was true, by the way) was all a part of my attempt to gain Franklin's trust. It would not do to tell him such a story that could easily be checked and found false. A creature like Joe Franklin gets spooked very easily, and I intended to instill in him a sense of trust, a sense that I was on his side. The politeness of thanking him for the articles he had sent regarding political, racial, and religious conspiracies was also intentional. It was all a part of the dance: build a rapport, share some inside jokes, agree on some subjects, and earn some trust. If we ever expected Joe to talk about anything other than his twisted delusions, we had to make him believe that it would benefit him to be straight with us. As long as he saw even the slightest possibility of a prison transfer on the horizon, and even better, if he believed that he could make us comfortable enough to let our guard down during that transfer, he would keep talking.

The newspaper clippings that Franklin had sent me included ads cut from various newspapers, ads that had been run by Larry Flynt's Campaign for the Office of President of the United States. He had also mailed to me some religious tracts written and published by "Christian Identity Preacher" Sheldon Emry. The tracts were racially biased and anti-Semitic in nature, the sort of stuff which had made Emry famous in some circles. Understand too, that these offerings were Franklin's attempt at building a rapport with me. I believe that he was also trying, once again, to justify his radical views, thereby justifying the actions he had taken to support them. That is just my opinion, but I believe that deep inside of him was a yearning to be understood, to gain a following, and ultimately to lead an uprising. He never missed an opportunity to spread his message of hate, even with me.

On the first of December, Franklin wrote a letter to me acknowledging receipt of mine to him. And this is where he and I began the
more intricate steps of the dance. He indicated that he had tried to
phone me at my office but hadn't been able to reach me, and that
he was ready to be truthful with me. He set the record straight on
a couple of issues, and he made some very specific requests in that
letter.

Joe asked me to arrange to send an attorney to Marion, saying
that he would like to talk to me through an attorney "about what
you asked about up here." He went on to say that his request had
nothing to do with the alleged contract placed on his life by Larry
Flynt, the dirty work supposedly to be done by his neighbor at
Marion, Mike Thevis.

"I made the whole thing up. I didn't really hear Thevis talking
about it on the phone. And don't waste your time getting that candy
analyzed. I broke the covering over it myself, you know? I was just
trying to figure out a way to get out of this place, away from Thevis
and the rest of these snitches and rats. I don't have a lot in common
with any of these low-life bastards, you know what I mean?"

Continuing, he wrote that he would like to transfer to a state
prison, maybe in North Dakota, Montana, or someplace, any place
"without niggers and Jews."

Now, the beat of the music was getting a little faster, the steps
a bit more complicated. Of course, there was a lot more to sending
an attorney to Marion than simply requesting one. In fact, since
Franklin hadn't officially been charged with a crime in Gwinnett
County, there was no way we could legally send an attorney to
Marion to talk to him about any alleged crime. Reading his admission about Thevis was interesting in that it indicated that he was
ready to have an honest (or as honest as was possible) conversation
with us. Of course, we seriously doubted all along the notion of
Mike Thevis being hired by Flynt to kill Franklin.

Having read and discussed Franklin's letter and requests, Mac,
Bruno, and I decided it was time to place a phone call to Franklin

at the prison in Marion. At around 2:00 p.m. on December 30, I made that call.

Of course, very early on, I advised Joe of two things. First, that our conversation was being recorded. Second, that if he intended to tell me anything that could be used against him, I had to read him his rights. He indulged me in the reading of his Miranda rights, then asked whether the radio he had playing in the background was too loud. I couldn't hear it at all, but he wanted to be sure that no one on his end was listening to what he was saying.

The first thing we discussed, after I read him his rights, was that I had asked the Gwinnett County District Attorney Bryant Huff about appointing an attorney for him as he had requested. As I suspected, the Superior Court Judge that Huff consulted said that he would not appoint a lawyer, as Franklin had not been charged with anything in Gwinnett County. I could not seek and retain a private attorney for him either, as that would cause the appearance of that attorney working with the police, not with him. In other words, if we retained an attorney for Franklin, or if we even became involved in that process in any manner, some defense attorney or appeals court could say that, since we were involved in retaining an attorney for Joe, then that attorney's allegiance was to us, not to him. The law is of course more complicated than I just explained it here, but that's the gist of it. If Franklin wanted an attorney, then he or a friend or family member would have to retain one. We could not. It would just look bad, if that makes sense.

Joe understood all of that; I suspect that he already knew our limitations when he made the request. Again though, I had to show him that I was "on his side," so to speak, that I was as good as my word. I had to make him believe that I was trying to help him out.

All of that out of the way, I asked him specifically about his claim that he had information about a case I was investigating, the Larry Flynt and Gene Reeves shooting five years earlier. I asked him point blank, "Did you shoot Larry Flynt?"

"Uh, no," he answered. "Actually it was another guy using my ID. Naw, just kidding. It was me."

I laughed at that answer. Guffawed, actually, even though his joke was obviously cavalier and inappropriate. It was in situations such as this one that I had to keep that tape rolling in the back of my mind the entire time I would talk with Joe. That's how I explained it anyway; other detectives used different coping mechanisms, I'm sure, but this was mine. I imagined a tape playing in the back of my mind during my conversations with Joe, one that reminded me that this was work, that I had to act like I was on his side even though the man and his beliefs and actions repulsed me. It's harder than you might think, to sit there and talk to a very dangerous man who would kill me in an instant if he had half a chance and thought it might benefit him. Franklin's thoughts and ideas were so strange, so crazy, that I had to keep at least one foot in what I knew to be reality. I hope that makes sense; it's the best way I can explain the odd duality of the situation in which I found myself on this case. It's tough, grueling, to converse and joke with a madman who is driven by white-hot hatred.

Once he made that admission to me, the one that confirmed he shot Flynt and Reeves, I explained to him that he wasn't the only person to claim responsibility for the shootings. Larry Flynt is a famous, flamboyant character, or at least he was back in the 1970s and '80s. Prison inmates, religious zealots, and people who just detested Flynt, *Hustler*, and everything in between had tried to take credit for the crime. When a sensational crime like the Flynt shooting happens, the crazies come out of the woodwork. It's an intriguing phenomenon and one you can bet on happening every single time. I suppose crazy attracts crazy, it's that simple.

I told Joe that I'd have to have proof, details that had not been released to the media, in order to take his admission seriously. I asked him to describe the scene of the shooting, where he had holed up, details such as those.

He proceeded to describe to me the interior of the abandoned building from which he shot the two men, the few things he remembered being inside it, even the greenish-colored "gunny sack" he had tacked over the front door. I asked him where he bought the tacks. He couldn't remember, and he asked me to jog his memory, by telling him whether they were white or silver.

"Now see, I can't answer that, Joe, because somebody could come back and say, 'Well, you told him that.' You follow what I'm talking about?"

He said that yes, he understood, then added that he had fired two shots from a .44 Marlin, ejected one cartridge, stuffed the gun back inside a pillowcase, and run out the back door. I knew that one Remington Peters .44 magnum shell casing had been found inside the abandoned house, right by the front doors. His statement about that one .44 magnum shell casing matched up with the fact that there were two shots fired, not three, as had been widely reported in the press. Of course, one bullet was removed from Flynt and one from Reeves. That knowledge had not been shared by the media, either. Joe described for me in great detail the route he took out of town. He couldn't remember all of the street names, but he described perfectly what he saw as he drove south—various landmarks, exits, and even restaurants and hotels. He told me that, once he was "pretty well clear of Lawrenceville," he pulled off the highway and made a phone call. I asked him who he called and what he said. He told me that he had been following the trial in the newspaper and knew that the case would have been sent to the jury on Monday, March 6. He called the courthouse and said that there wouldn't be any use sending the case to the jury, because Jesus Christ had already taken care of it. "The chick hung up before I got to finish my statement, or she went to get someone else and I hung up," he added. "I don't remember which one of us hung up first, but it was quick."

When I asked him where he stayed when he was in town in March of '78, he said that he was staying at a little motel off I-85, south of Gwinnett County, and that he had registered under the name of James A. Cooper.

"Which motel?"

"Ah . . . I forget the name of that sucker."

"What was it near?"

Joe then described to me where the Holiday Inn was, the one in which Flynt, his lawyers, and companions were staying, near Lawrenceville along I-85. "I kept that place under really close surveillance, you know, for a long time . . . but he moved from there, to somewhere else . . . but I stayed in that little motel the whole time. Right now, I can't recall the exact name of it. If I saw it or saw the name, I could remember it."

I knew that this would be a sticking point, a critical piece of information. If we could go through the motel's March 1978 register and find the name "James A. Cooper," then we'd have something solid, something that put Joe in the area at that time. I kept pushing.

"Can you describe the area?"

He thought aloud, recalling that there was a Denny's restaurant nearby. "Shallowford Road, I think that's the name of the road it's on."

That was good. A possible road name and a nearby business. That narrowed the location down for us. I asked him what he did with the gun.

"Yeah, I got rid of it. Uh, I just took it and uh, cut it . . . took it all apart and disposed of it in various places. The wood stock and all that, I got rid of it in a dumpster."

"You didn't sell it?" My research had turned up the fact that Joe bought, sold, and stole guns regularly. If he had sold it, we could very possibly track the sale. The task would be daunting, but it was possible.

"I didn't sell that one, no. I cut the barrel off that sucker, you know, and took a pipe cutter, and cut the barrel in half. I took it and buried it."

"Where did you get it from?" I asked.

"Let's see, I think I stole that gun. Yeah, I ripped it off from somebody."

That was another key point we'd have to pin down. I asked him where he was when he stole it, and where he buried it. He remembered clearly that he buried the gun somewhere along Buford Highway, out near a Gwinnett city named Lilburn. He was fuzzy on the exact location, but then he threw in the fact that he had come back to the town square in Gwinnett and driven past the old rock building a year or two after the shooting. "I was out there just cruising around, ya know, checking out the scene again. The Mormons took that building over, ya know. They remodeled the whole thing, and there's a sign over it that says 'Church of Jesus Christ of Latter Day Saints.'" He kept talking on that point; he seemed to be fascinated with the reminiscence. "There was boards in the back of the house, near the back door."

Describing how he had originally entered the building when he was scoping it out for the shooting, he said that he had to climb through a window. Once inside, he pried open the back door, which had made his escape much faster. I knew that part was true.

"What kind of shoes were you wearing?"

"Adidas. Size ten and a half. I threw them away, because my prints were all over the dirt on the floor and in the dirt outside." That part was true, also. I had read about the shoe prints in the crime scene investigation report, as well as the forensics report.

I went back to the gun. "Do you remember where you stole it?" He said that he stole it in Alabama, somewhere near Birmingham. He just happened to see it in a truck and took it. I told him that I needed an exact place. I needed a jurisdiction in which I could find a report of the incident. He couldn't remember. He hadn't stolen it specifically to shoot Larry Flynt, he said. He had had it for a couple of years before doing that.

I asked him if he had gone anywhere else in the vacant house besides the room from which he shot. He said that he had, and I asked him to describe it to me. He did, and fairly accurately. He then volunteered the fact that he had actually gone over to the state courthouse on the town square, keeping it under surveillance to see when Flynt came and went, and where he went when he left the building. He had seen on the front door that the judge was G. Hughell Harrison. That was correct. He could have read that somewhere, but I doubted that he'd remember it all these years later. If I'm not mistaken, he even spelled the name properly when I asked him to.

And then, he told me something that was chilling, something that gave me a brief glimpse into the absolute evil that was in Joe Franklin. He told me that he was inside the abandoned building, checking the vantage point, becoming familiar with the ambush spot and the flow of both car and foot traffic. Two women walked by; he could hear them talking from inside the building. "So I thought I'd just go ahead and practice, and as they walked by, I'd get a bead on them just, ya know, to get ready for the real thing." I imagined the two innocent women, and how their lives could so easily have been cut short if he had just chosen to take a couple of practice shots. Of course, he didn't do that for obvious reasons, but who can predict what a madman will do on any given day? Had the man holding that rifle been so inclined, he could have erased those women from the earth with no more effort or regret than another man might shoot a pigeon or a rabbit.

And with stunning indifference, Joe described to me the actual shooting. He remembered minute details, such as the gray granite curb and wall along Perry Street. He described the sounds Flynt made as he grabbed his stomach, dropping in the street and eventually, not making a sound at all as he slipped into shock, his dark blood leaking and pooling on the black asphalt. "I figured he was dead, so I left."

As he was running out the back door, he remembered hearing Flynt moan again, and he thought, "Crap, man. He isn't even dead." At about that same time, he heard tires squealing, so he just kept on running out the door and to his car. Later, he learned that the squealing tires belonged to the black and silver Camaro that onlookers had described fleeing the scene. The car had nothing to do with the crime; it was just a lucky break, a distraction that had confused eyewitnesses.

I told him that I wasn't absolutely sure that everything he had told me hadn't been reported in a newspaper somewhere along the way. I pushed for more specifics, asking him what kind of ammunition he had used. Without hesitation, he answered, "240 grain solid point. They weren't hollow points. I just had some, a little bit left in a box." The ammunition had indeed been solid point, and I felt sure that that piece of information had not been publicized.

Then, another piece of random information: "I do remember being in Bexley, Ohio, at some point. Ever heard of it?" I answered no, that I had never heard of the town.

"It's a suburb of Columbus. That's where Flynt used to live at. I hit that bank there, remember I told you that? While I was there, I called up his house, and I said, 'Is Larry Flynt there?' And they said no, he was in the Bahamas, so I just hung up." Joe went on to say that he had actually staked out Flynt's house in Ohio several times, even using a telescope to look into the windows one November night in 1977. "Then, I read in the newspaper that he would be in Lawrenceville for the trial." He didn't know exactly where Lawrenceville was, but he knew he had been in the area buying the Gran Torino not long before he read that article. And that's when he decided to shoot Flynt in Georgia.

I want to take a moment here to reiterate that Joe was able to commit so many murders, bank robberies, and bombings without getting caught, and he did this for three years. Those are all major crimes, ones that draw the attention of law enforcement agencies. To commit so many of them without getting caught was quite a feat. Joe admitted to killing (as best he could guess) twenty-two people. He admitted this to me as well as to reporters with whom he spoke just before he was executed. He committed at least sixteen bank robberies, and he bombed several synagogues. He even claimed to have raped a woman just before his killing spree began. He got away with these things for so long because of one tactic in particular. He would commit a crime, and then he wouldn't surface again until he was somewhere four- or five-hundred miles away. He never stayed in the same location as a crime he just committed for very long; he would pull up stakes and travel like that immediately, as soon as he pulled the trigger or took the money. He had absolutely no ties to anyone or any place. Even in 1979 at age twenty-eight, when he married sixteen-year-old Anita Carden in DeKalb County, Georgia, Joe Franklin had no ties to anyone, not even his young wife. The couple had a child within about a year, and still he had no ties. You see, Joe Franklin was so focused, so dedicated, to his hate campaign that his own wife and daughter seemed to serve as distractions, and he told so many lies to Anita that, while she thought she knew him, she didn't. She had no idea who she was married to. Joe even used one of his favorite aliases, James A. Cooper, on their marriage license. Yes, Anita knew her husband as James Cooper, not Jimmy Vaughn or Joseph Franklin.

Jimmy and Anita met in an ice cream shop, and began dating right away. With her parents' permission, they married and stayed married about a year, just long enough to make a child, a little girl named Lori. Anita said later, when newspaper and magazine reporters practically stood in line for the chance to interview her in the early '80s, that he had changed, had become angry and secretive shortly after they married. His mood could become dark without any notice at all, and during those times her husband was simply unreachable. Not too long after they both said "I do," the beatings began. She divorced him, not only because of his anger and violence; he had also had sexual relations with a prostitute just a few months into the marriage, and Anita had found out about it. At age sixteen, a young, gullible Anita Carden had married James A. Cooper (at least, that was the name he wrote on their marriage license), a solemn, sad, often angry "plumber" who used to travel for work for weeks at a time. When he came home, he would have thousands of dollars in his pocket, enough to pay the rent and buy groceries for a month or two, sometimes with a little bit left over. During those times, the young couple would go to a movie or spend time together doing the things that young couples do, before the pressures of children and career choke out the luxury of carefree dating. She never thought to question the lies that he had told her; they were layered so thick and so deep that sometimes even he had a hard time telling truth from fiction. James A. Cooper was not really James A. Cooper at all. He was Jimmy Vaughn, then Joseph Franklin. He was not a plumber either, and when he traveled, it was not to do any plumbing. He was a murderer, filled with hate. He robbed banks for money, and the FBI and other law enforcement agencies were starting to sniff around. Still, the young wife had no idea who and what her husband was. She divorced him a disappointed but much wiser young woman, and the mother of a daughter. Anita never really understood who Joe Franklin, a.k.a. James A. Cooper, a.k.a. Jimmy Vaughn and many more, was until years after they parted.

At any rate, Joe and I continued our conversation for a while longer. I tried to nail him down to specifics about his purchase of the Gran Torino—names, dates, things like that. I went back to the theft of the rifle, pressing him to remember a city so that I could verify the theft by finding a police report. I pushed him to remember where he had buried the parts of the gun after he had cut it up. At about that time, a guard came in and told Joe that he had two more minutes on the phone. I decided to ask him a question of crucial importance.

"Joe, why did you shoot Larry Flynt?"

"I just wanted to try to wipe ... I just hated the crap I used to see in that *Hustler* magazine, ya know? I hated the race mixing. They would degrade white women in there all the time. And ah, they were ... like I was telling you, every time I read ... I would go check out that magazine in downtown Atlanta.

"Every time you would turn around, they would have a picture of a white woman giving a blow job to some nigger or Jew, or everything from an Eskimo to an African. I just hated the way they would degrade white women in that magazine."

I left the question at that, telling him that I was going to start tracking down the name of the motel, the people who had sold him the Gran Torino, and find all the evidence I could so that I could take it all to the DA and compare it to what he had told me. He asked if I thought that then, they would appoint him an attorney. I said that I hoped so, though I secretly doubted it. We then set up a time to talk via telephone the following week, and Joe said he'd try to think of more details about the gun, the car, and any other circumstances that could verify what he'd confessed to.

The time, the man-hours, and the footwork required to chase down details of gun sales, car sales, and such are grueling. They require patience, skill, and a very fine-toothed comb. Remember, this was a time that was pre-Internet. It was pre-anything, really, except for telephones, card files, and microfiche. We had our work cut out for us. Dan Bruno and I spent hours looking through issues of Atlanta trade magazines, those that advertised cars for sale, guns for sale, anything a person might need. I believe the main one was called the Atlanta Trader, or something like that. We'd find an ad, call the number listed (five years after an ad runs, the phone number is probably disconnected or under someone else's name), try to find the new number if the first one was no good, track down the new number, and so on. It was tedious work, and we didn't have secretaries or assistants to help us with it. I wish I knew how many hours we spent in the dark, dank basement of the local library, trying to carefully walk the same steps that Joe Franklin had walked five years ago. This was all a part of the effort to prove or disprove Joe's claims, to thoroughly exhaust all other possibilities and explanations, in order that we might prove him to be the man who shot attorney and client as they strolled through Lawrenceville on that sunny day in March, 1978.

CHAPTER 18
A Second Visit
(July 1984)

Detective Michael Cowart

While Joe and I continued our correspondence through the mail well into 1984, he had become less forthcoming with specifics about the Larry Flynt shooting. When we spoke on the telephone at his request (I could no longer initiate conversations, since he had made it known that he wanted an attorney), he refused to allow me to tape the conversations. "Every time I allow somebody to record me, the tape ends up in the hands of the Feds," he complained. I resorted to taking handwritten notes when we'd talk, but as I mentioned, Joe was intentionally withholding information. He was not getting what he wanted, which, as I've stated, was a transfer to another prison. We continued in that cagey manner for a few months, keeping the lines of communication open, but I was not getting anything helpful from him any longer. I needed specifics and details that would help me prove that he did, in fact, shoot Larry Flynt and Gene Reeves.

Then on July 19, 1984, I received a letter at the Police Department, addressed to me from Joseph Paul Franklin. In that letter, he stated, "I have some more information about the Flynt case I remembered, and which I haven't given to you yet. There is also an incident where camera crews that were in the area (on March 6, 1978) got me on film near the Lawrenceville courthouse. If you could bring a tape recorder up here, I would like to discuss it with you." He also took the liberty of including a pamphlet entitled "How They Rule: The Media Monopolies that Rule America," reprinted from the National Vanguard. Basically, the pamphlet explained how the media in the United States is controlled by Jews. And just like that, we were back in business.

Bruno and I requested permission to visit Franklin at Marion again, and permission was granted. Mac had another commitment, so this time it would be Dan Bruno and me. On Thursday, August 16, 1984, I again stepped into the unnerving quiet of Marion, this time with Bruno at my side. He felt the same about the spit-shined, polished cleanliness and deafening quiet of the prison as I did: uncomfortable and intimidated.

The security measures that applied when Mac and I had interviewed Franklin last fall still applied. We would be escorted deep into the bowels of the prison and locked in a room with Franklin for four hours.

By about 12:45 p.m., all three of us were sitting in a room together. This time, we were meeting in the Special Unit Library and exercise room. I'm not sure why we were given different accommodations this trip, but I did not ask. I knew I could rest assured that every decision made at Marion was made for a reason, with the safety of guards, visitors, and of course prisoners at the core of that decision.

I introduced Franklin and Bruno, we all shook hands as best we could given the restrictive hardware that encumbered Joe, then took our seats. I pulled a small voice recorder out of the pocket of my trousers, and Franklin protested immediately. For the same reason he had given me before when I asked to record our telephone conversations, he would not allow it now. The move didn't surprise me, even though he had asked me to bring a voice recorder. That was how Joe worked. He probably knew we wouldn't have been so quick to agree to another meeting without the ability to record the conversation. He had no objection, however, to my taking notes. For about an hour, Bruno and I listened to the man sitting across from us rant and preach about his political views, as well as his interpretation of the Bible.

When he did get around to discussing the Flynt shooting, he laughed good-naturedly and said that he had seriously considered playing a whopper of a joke on us. He had planned to make a statement claiming that congressman Larry McDonald and others had paid him to shoot Flynt. Still laughing, he added that he intended to throw in some facts and details, to make his claim sound genuine. For example, Joe said that he had once gotten the clap in Atlanta and had to go to a urologist to clear it up. To his great delight (so he claims), the urologist who treated him was Larry McDonald's father. Bruno and I politely smiled at his clever joke, and I secretly hoped that this visit wasn't going to be a complete waste of our time. I also had to wonder, had he picked up a newspaper or magazine and read some of Flynt's bizarre opinions about conspiracies behind his shooting? Is that where he learned of Flynt's theory about McDonald being involved in a contract hit on Flynt's life? I couldn't be sure of anything, really, when embroiled in a conversation with Franklin. I made a note to see what, if anything, had been printed about Larry McDonald in connection with Larry Flynt. He then made reference to his claim that Billy Carter had hired him to shoot Flynt. "I was just having a good time with those stories. They wasn't true. But I was going to pin it on McDonald, just to see the look on your face. Ah, but I couldn't do that to you."

He laughed for a minute or two longer, then chuckled, and then all traces of humor faded from his face as he looked straight at Bruno. "It's true. I shot Larry Flynt. I acted alone, and it was racially motivated. That bastard was always race-mixing in *Hustler* magazine, and I wanted to wipe it clean." Then, as if he had been studying to take a test on which his life depended, Joe began reciting facts and details that he couldn't seem to remember before. He remembered details about the store from which he bought the thumbtacks. He even drew the layout of the store, but he refused to draw any diagrams on paper, so he drew on his palm. He didn't want his drawings falling into the hands of the Feds either, I suppose. He drew (again, on his palm), a diagram of the interior of the building from which he shot Flynt. He mentioned a closet in which he stashed the thumbtacks; when I asked him where the closet was inside the house, he said that he "had to hold a few things back" for when he got down to Georgia. Then, he'd tell us everything. Always playing a game of chess. Always maneuvering.

He recounted his 1977 surveillance of *Hustler* headquarters in Columbus, Ohio, near the corner of Gay and High Streets. He remembered exact details of street layouts in the area, the building locations, and even the placement of surveillance cameras on the property. "I planned to plug him then," he said. But for one reason or another, that plan fell through. Sometimes Joe would say that it was because Flynt was away in the Bahamas. Sometimes he would claim that it was too hard to get to him. To this day, the reason is unclear to me. All that matters is that he did, indeed, stalk and shoot Flynt and Reeves in Gwinnett County, Georgia, the next year. I believe that with all my heart.

After a couple of hours, Franklin stated that he was tired and did not want to talk any more. I turned the conversation to Joseph Kitts, who Franklin dismissed as a drunk. When we asked him whether he had buried stolen guns where Kitts claimed that he had, he stammered and hesitated, then answered that he had buried some guns under that particular railroad bridge, but maybe not the ones stolen from the Athens, Georgia, gun shop.

Joe then turned the conversation to an article he had read in *Hustler* magazine after the Flynt shooting, one written by Jim Nygaard, a *Hustler* staff attorney. He pointed out several inaccuracies in the article, including Nygaard's statement that there were three shots fired, and not two. His knowledge of the specifics of the event, in my mind, was further proof that he committed the crime.

He did go on to say that he did not shoot anyone in Wisconsin, nor did he bomb any synagogue in Chattanooga. The rest of our time was spent listening to more of his convoluted interpretations of the Bible. I have no doubt that he made those claims of innocence in Wisconsin and Tennessee with some manipulation and purpose in mind, and I thought to myself, *How does he keep all the lies straight?* In the end, though, I don't believe it mattered whether he kept them straight. Joe would say whatever he thought was necessary to achieve his ultimate purpose (duplicity, manipulation, and escape, always escape), and he didn't have to keep the lies straight, or prove or disprove them. He had attorneys to do that.

CHAPTER 19
The Fall
(1980)

WHILE AT THE detention center in Kentucky, Franklin turned on his good old boy charm, making easy conversation with his captors while they questioned him, served him coffee, and searched his stolen vehicle. While Joe was inside the jail chatting up the officers and drinking steaming hot java, two officers outside the building were cataloguing quite an impressive cache of firearms in the trunk of the impounded car, and of course the one weapon in the back seat. The two men knew that they had stumbled onto something big; neither of them had ever seen so many high-powered firearms in the possession of one man. That's saying an awful lot, considering the fact that Kentucky boasts of some of the best hunting in the country.

At about the same time that the two cops were handling his shotguns and handguns out back, Joe excused himself from the friendly conversation in the break room of the Florence, Kentucky, police department. "I have to go take a leak," he said to the officer sitting closest to him, and he was escorted to the men's room. The officer stood outside the door while Joe went about his business. "No funny business now," the officer warned his prisoner, and both men chuckled good-naturedly at the very thought. *Funny business, indeed. We're all good friends now, buddy.* As soon as the door whispered closed, however, Joe's smile disappeared without a trace, and he looked around the tiny tiled room for a way out. There were two stalls and two urinals, and over the urinals was a small window. Working quickly, he flushed one of the toilets, turned on the water at the single sink in the bathroom, and climbed atop a urinal. He cranked the window open; it would be a tight fit but luckily, he was in pretty good shape. He pulled himself up and stuck his head out the small window to see if anyone was looking. Seeing no one, he pulled and squeezed until he tumbled out the other side onto the ground several feet below. He got to his feet (there wasn't a scratch on him), looked both ways again, and began walking quickly, then running as fast as he could, away from the Florence police department, away from his new buddies and the hot coffee at the break room table, and away from that fucking nosy cop who spotted the rifle on the back seat of his car at the diner. He was free, but he had left his car (and the firearms that were in it) behind. The car was stolen, as were most of the guns, but he had purchased some of the weapons using several false identities, and a couple of those were in the glove box. He was sure of it. His fingerprints were all over the weapons, and he knew that. He knew enough to know that his fingerprints would tie all the aliases together, and that would be bad for him. Within a half hour of his clumsy but effective escape, a national manhunt for Joseph Paul Franklin had been issued. Now, he had the FBI's full attention.

During the five hours he spent with the Florence police officers, he learned that he was wanted for questioning in the deaths of the two young men in Salt Lake City. He also learned that the FBI wanted to talk to him about several other crimes, including the Indiana shooting of Vernon Jordan, the shooting deaths of a black man and a white woman in Pennsylvania, the shooting deaths of two black Cincinnati youths, and a black man and white woman in Oklahoma City. There was enough evidence found in his car to lend credence to what had before just been long-shot suppositions of his guilt in several crimes, both murders and bank robberies. He knew that the trusting but eager Kentucky officers had found all of his guns by now, and he had to assume that the guns were being traced, notes compared, fingerprints lifted, and phone calls made. He also had to assume that they were highly pissed off that he had made such fools of them, and that they would be hot on his trail by now.

It had all seemed so insignificant. He had just ducked inside the diner to grab a bite to eat but then, so had the brown-nosing cop. Leaving that gun on the seat in plain view was a big mistake, one that he was not often guilty of making. That one slip-up would cost him dearly; his escape from the friendly officers at the detention center in Kentucky just sweetened the pot for local and federal lawmen alike. Cuffing Joe Franklin, especially now, would earn some cop somewhere a nice little bonus and a promotion. Franklin would have to be extra careful, because not only had he killed a lot of people and robbed dozens of banks, but also because he had embarrassed those hick cops in Kentucky. Cops didn't like to be embarrassed. *I been doing it for years. I know.*

While Franklin was both surprised and flattered to hear that his name was now being connected to racially motivated murders, he was also proud that the high and mighty FBI was finally looking at him as being a possible suspect. *It's about damn time. What do I have to do, send them photos and confessions?* Publicity and media coverage were exactly what he needed to jump start a race war. It had frustrated him for years that the media would not report his missions. In his opinion, they were too scared to publicize his deeds. These days, everybody was too scared to say anything to or about the niggers. It was possible too, that the federal government was suppressing the stories for its own purposes. He didn't know why his missions weren't making the newspapers or national news shows, but he had his suspicions, and they all boiled down to some kind of conspiracy. *I'll just keep on killing 'til they have no choice but to pay attention. I'm doing the country and the white race a service. Someday, they'll thank me.*

During his brief but pleasant stay in the Florence, Kentucky, detention center, Joe heard another bit of news that piqued his interest. That very summer, black children down in Atlanta were being murdered left and right, and so far, no arrests had been made. Of course, he had been following the story in the *Atlanta Journal Constitution*, but while he was in the custody of the Florence cops, he learned for the first time of the reward money.

Atlanta's mayor Maynard Jackson had recently been photographed surrounded by several security guards and standing behind stacks of cash—$150,000 in reward money for anyone who could offer information leading to the arrest and conviction of the child murderer. It had been a long, hot summer in Atlanta, and the mounting body count of Atlanta's murdered inner-city children rose with the mercury. Panic and hysteria were gaining a foothold in the city, and municipal officials as well as citizens were demanding that heads roll. There were accusations by leaders in the black community that Atlanta cops were indifferent to the murders, refusing to vigorously pursue the killer because the victims were black children. There were accusations by some in the white community that the crimes were black-on-black, committed for the sole purpose of inciting a race riot. In the South, the wheel goes 'round and 'round, and in the summer of 1980, racial tensions were thick. Atlanta was as shaky and unstable as a pile of old, sweaty dynamite that year. Someone would have to answer for the killings, and soon.

Franklin, interested solely in the reward money, might have been surprised to learn that his name was on a list of several that the FBI was compiling as being possible perpetrators of the Atlanta child murders. That notion might have offended someone else, but not Joe. He was proud of the fact that his name was finally being associated with racial hatred, even if the FBI was a mile away from the truth. He hadn't been in Atlanta murdering children of any color. He had been too busy on the road for all that. Besides, if the FBI knew as much about him as they thought they did, they'd have known that he'd never stick around one place for an entire summer. It was habits like that that got a man caught.

A young black man named Wayne Williams was eventually blamed for committing most of the Atlanta child murders that took place between 1979 and 1981. In 1982, he was tried and convicted of killing two adult men, and that conviction earned him life imprisonment. After that trial and sentencing, the Atlanta police department announced that Williams was responsible for at least twenty-three of the twenty-nine child murders, but he has never been formally indicted, nor has he ever been tried for any of them. His guilt has been disputed by many, and a cloud of suspicion still hangs over the announcement, a cloud that some called "too convenient." Some blacks maintained that blaming a black man for the murders of so many black children was purely white strategy, taking race out of the equation altogether and thereby avoiding the inevitable backlash of protests and rioting had a white perpetrator been named. Williams himself, to this day, maintains his innocence.

It seemed that in the late '60s, '70s and even the early '80s, the South was in a valley of strife, death, and hatred. It was one of those inevitable cycles in time that exacted payment toward the staggering debt of past crimes, for which She is ultimately responsible. There is blood in the Southern soil, and it will likely never be washed clean.

Franklin had wished he had a name to give them down there in Atlanta, because he sure could use that $150,000. There's a lot of truth to the old adage that "there is no honor among thieves." He might have named his own child as the perpetrator if he thought that doing so would get him $150,000. He was now a fugitive from the law, a wanted man most definitely on law enforcement's radar, and robbing a bank right now for some quick cash was out of the question. Flat broke and on the run from Utah and Kentucky authorities, as well as from the FBI and God knew who else, he'd have to turn to the only other means of making money that he knew, and that was donating blood.

Without a car in the days following his escape, Franklin hitch-hiked several miles down south, then took a calculated risk and stole a car to travel the rest of the way to Florida. As he traveled, law enforcement officers back in Kentucky were gathering enough evidence from his car to link him to several sniper-style killings. The Feds issued a national alert to homeless shelters and blood banks, tipping off workers and volunteers to be on the lookout for Franklin. His hair color changed several times a month. In fact, his hair was falling out in chunks as a result of the constant bleaching and dyeing. But his body art never changed, except that later in life it had faded as he sat rotting in jail with those he saw as lowlifes and losers, who he detested so much. Descriptions and images of his distinctive and sometimes crude tattoos were dead giveaways to his identity.

Down in Georgia, Detective Michael Cowart studied news footage from other states, clips that detailed sniper-style murders that smacked of racism. He read FBI reports (scarce as they were—those boys were stingy with their information), as well as news-paper clippings and alerts, and he and his team had been doing homework of their own. The FBI never kept the detectives down in Georgia in the loop, that much was for sure. For a long time, any information Cowart, Bruno, and McKelvey compiled regarding Joseph Paul Franklin, they got on their own.

Franklin, until recently thought to be no more than a down-on-his-luck petty criminal and general nuisance, was taking on the unmistakable shape of a shrewd and cunning serial murderer and bank robber.

On October 28, 1980, just a few weeks after the FBI alert was issued, Joseph Franklin walked into Sera-Tec, a blood bank in Lakeland, Florida. He registered under an assumed name, gave up a pint of his blood, collected his cash, and walked out into the warm Florida sunshine. He didn't notice the young medical technician in the lab motioning to another, then stepping quietly into a small office, closing the door behind him to place a phone call. He didn't notice the nervous glances between workers as he drank his orange juice and gingerly peeled off the bandage placed in the crook of his arm just minutes ago. He just knew that he had enough cash to buy food for a couple of days; that was all that mattered right now. He thanked the young girl who carefully counted out the cash, placing it in his hand as she did so. "Five, ten, fifteen, twenty. . ." she recited, glancing nervously at her supervisor while she counted. Within just forty-five minutes of his arrival at the Lakeland blood bank, Joe Franklin exited the small, concrete building, glancing left, then right, then stopping mid-step as he counted his cash. Something didn't feel right.

Six FBI agents greeted him as he left the building, guns drawn, instructing him to get on his knees and place his hands atop his head. "Get on your knees. NOW!" one of the men yelled at the top of his lungs, and their guns remained trained on his head and his chest.

Though the thought of running briefly crossed his mind as he slowly lowered himself to his knees, he knew without a doubt that this time, there would be no escape.

On October 31, 1980, a federal jury in Utah indicted Franklin for violating the civil rights of Fields and Martin, the two joggers he murdered in cold blood in Liberty Park. On November 7, he was extradited to Salt Lake City and arraigned for the murders of joggers Ted Fields and David Martin. His bail was set at one million dollars. The following year, in March, he was tried and convicted of violating the civil rights of Fields and Martin and received two consecutive life sentences. Three months later, he was convicted of actually killing both men; as the result of a hung jury that could have handed down the death penalty, Franklin received two more life sentences. It was during the sentencing phase of this trial that he escaped, only to be recaptured on a different floor of the courthouse a few hours later. Not long after that conviction, other states began lining up to prosecute him for sniper shootings, licking their chops and tuning up their electric chairs. They'd have to stand in line to get a piece of him, but they were making the connections all the same. If there's one thing cops hate, it's an unsolved case.

On January 31, 1982, Joseph Franklin was transferred to the federal penitentiary at Marion, Illinois, to begin serving his life sentences. Three days after entering Marion, he was attacked by a group of black inmates and stabbed fifteen times. His reputation had apparently preceded him. This attack, and the fact that he had proved himself to be a slippery character and shameless opportunist, got him transferred to the control unit at Marion—a prison within the prison. In that unit, any hope of escape withered and died. Even Joe Franklin couldn't pull off such a feat from the infamous Belly of the Beast.

Franklin's three-year legacy of murder and robbery had finally ended that October of 1980, with his quiet and uneventful arrest outside a Florida blood bank.

Ultimately, Joseph Paul Franklin was handed six life sentences by the time everybody was done with him. That may sound like a lot, but he admitted to "about" twenty-two killings, give or take a couple, over the three-year span of his crusade. Many jurisdictions, and Georgia was among them, made the decision not to prosecute Franklin because frankly, there was no point to it. He would never live long enough to get out of Marion; the only way he'd be leaving there would be if another state was ready and willing to kill him for his transgressions. Prosecuting him in Georgia back then would have cost taxpayers about $50,000 by most estimates. There was also the spectacle that such a trial would generate for the district attorney to consider. The security, the media frenzy, and the payoff for prosecuting him in Georgia and other states that were waiting their turns just didn't stack up to the logistics nightmare and cost to taxpayers. And always, there was the possibility of an escape. If anyone could pull off an escape even under the tightest of security, it was Joe Franklin.

Ultimately, Franklin was indicted but not tried for the shootings of Gene Reeves and Larry Flynt.

He was tried in August 1982 for violating the civil rights of Vernon Jordan, and found not guilty. Over the next couple of years, Franklin confessed to shooting Jordan, Larry Flynt, and Gene Reeves, as well as more than a dozen other victims. He confessed to the Chattanooga synagogue bombing, and to two murders in Wisconsin (and for his trouble there, received two more life sentences). There was a method to his madness, because confessions meant additional trials, and additional trials meant transfers to other states for the proceedings. A transfer out of Marion to undergo another trial was worth the risk of another conviction, even in a death penalty state. The risk was justified primarily because he hated Marion, but also because a transfer was simply another opportunity to escape. All totaled, Joe Franklin was convicted of killing eight people, though he admitted to twenty-two, "give or take a few" (in his own words).

In 1994, he confessed to the 1977 killing of Gerald Gordon, the Jewish man whose only crime had been leaving a synagogue in Missouri. Joe said that he committed the crime because he was told in a dream to do so. In 1997, he was convicted of killing Gordon, and shortly thereafter, he was moved from his hated home in Marion to the prison in Bonne Terre, Missouri. Court transcripts reflect the fact that Franklin stated in open court that his only regret concerning the killing was that "it was illegal to kill niggers and Jews." He asked the Missouri jurors to give him the death penalty and when they obliged, he gave them a satisfied "thumbs up."

CHAPTER 20

A Tangled Web
(1983)

Detective Michael Cowart

I suppose the defining moment for me came during the Cincinnati conference, when local law enforcement came together to share information on a serial violent criminal. Later, the FBI would claim credit for the conference as being their idea but in reality, it was the joint effort of local jurisdictions intent on piecing together a nationwide puzzle that would hopefully ensnare a vicious serial killer. It was during that conference and the subsequent research that I came to realize that Joseph Paul Franklin was the genuine article, not a want-to-be, not a spur-of-the-moment opportunist, and not a casual criminal. He was as hardened a criminal as I had ever encountered. One of the points that helped me come to this awakening was the shared fact that he would commit a crime and the next day turn up five hundred miles away, likely committing another crime. When you think about it, not many people are pre-pared or willing to live a life like that. It's that mobility, that absence of ties, that makes a criminal very hard to catch. Even the worst of the worst criminals has a mama they touch base with, or a wife or girlfriend that he just can't stay away from. Not this man. He had no one, and he lived that life intentionally. He, the very idea of him, was a little frightening, even to seasoned professionals like Dan, Mac, and me.

The dominoes that supported the building of cases against Franklin began to tumble when a police captain at that Cincinnati conference slipped out of session a little early and made a bee line for the press. He described, in great detail, the theories and suppositions that had been discussed (and that's mostly what they were at the time, theories and suppositions). This insight made newspaper headlines in several cities and touched off a firestorm of interviews, confessions, manipulations, and dangled carrots. Law enforcement officials in several states were beginning to connect the dots with respect to bank robberies, murders, and bombings and Joe Franklin, always one to figure out an angle that benefitted his purposes, began to use their eagerness to his advantage. If he confessed just enough details to just the right people, someone would get hungry enough to pull some strings and get him out of Marion, if only for a trial. The FBI would have to authorize a transfer, but he couldn't get them to talk to him, no matter what he confessed. No, he'd have to get the attention of the smaller jurisdictions, and they could go begging the FBI for the chance to get a shot at the man who had eluded them so cleverly for all these years. All he needed was a minute or two with a guard who wasn't paying attention, and he'd be out again, furthering his crusade. I don't believe for one second that he ever lost sight of that mission, or his passion for inciting a race war.

Of course, when word got out from the Cincinnati conference, and when the media began circulating stories based on the police captain's leaked information, Larry Flynt got wind of the news that a lone, racist drifter had admitted to trying to kill him. For whatever reason, the flamboyant publisher initially rejected the notion, lock, stock and barrel.

He arranged a July 30, 1984, interview with WGST radio in Atlanta, a news talk radio show. At the time, WGST was a dominant news source for metropolitan Atlanta. The purpose of the interview was twofold. First, Flynt used the format to promote his candidacy for president of the United States. During the interview, he explained his platform and his stance on certain issues. Second, he revealed that he had in his possession information as to who was really behind the March 6, 1978, shooting. I will say this for the man—he could sound very convincing, even if he might have been telling a blatant lie.

In October of that same year, "Mac" McKelvey went to the WGST radio station studio and secured a copy of the tape from that July interview. He and I listened to that taped interview, then spent weeks slogging through the subsequent research that was necessary to confirm or negate claims made in that interview. With his claims and accusations, Flynt opened up a can of worms in the truest sense of the words. Joe Franklin was a liar; we already knew that to be true. But based on our research, Larry Flynt also appeared to be a manipulator, or at the very least a man who had been terribly misled by a troupe of liars.

The name of the WGST radio show was "Counterpoint." As Mac and I listened to the tape, Host Tom Houck welcomed Flynt to the show and as soon as the pornographer announced his candidacy and presented his platform, Houck got right to the meat of things. He pointed out early on that Flynt did not believe that Franklin was the man who shot him in Gwinnett County six years earlier.

Flynt, in his undiluted Kentucky accent made more syrupy by neurological damage, agreed with Houck. "I'm not saying he might not o' had something to do with it, but I know he wasn't the man who shot me. I know that [D.A.] Bryant Huff knows this, too. And look, the people in Georgia involved in my shooting know who they were, and, uh, eventually they're all going to pay for it too." The publisher then went on to claim that he had a signed confession in his hands, one made by a man named Rich Richardson. He referred to Richardson as a "bag man," the man who had amassed some $25,000 and then gave that money to a man named Clark Williams.

In his signed confession, according to Flynt, Richardson admitted to having the firearm used in the shooting and that the man who had shot both Flynt and Reeves was Clark Williams. Then, Flynt went on to name several Georgia politicians who, he alleged, had put a contract and a price on his head: Al Burris (a senator from Cobb County and Senate majority leader), Tom Murphy (speaker of the Georgia House), Culver Kidd (senator from Milledgeville, Georgia), Newt Gingrich (US representative from Cobb County), and Larry McDonald (member, US House of Representatives, and cousin of General George Patton).

Of course, once Flynt made the claims that he did during that interview, the responsibility fell to us to investigate them.

The first thing we did was to call the Flynt Publication Corporation in California. We spoke with Mr. Bill Ryder, the corporation's Director of Security. He seemed surprised to hear about the WGST interview and was not able to offer any information about the claims made by Flynt. We then asked to speak to Flynt himself, and Ryder transferred the call. When he answered, I remember thinking to myself that Flynt sounded as though he was under the influence of a heavy narcotic when he spoke to us that day. I do not know whether he was, or whether the residual neurological damage he suffered from the shooting affected his speech in that manner. He sounded a bit more slurry than he had during the radio interview. He confirmed that he had a signed confession from Richardson, and he stated that the Georgia politicians named earlier had contributed the money to have him shot. When we asked him whether we could see this signed confession, he said that if he had to produce the document, he'd "come up with something." Right then and there, it appeared to us as if he had no such document.

We did our homework though, and we found a man named Rich Richardson; he was an accomplished con artist who already had a record with the Gwinnett County police department. We found no information on him that even remotely connected him to

Flynt or to a "Clark Williams," the supposed gunman whose existence we never verified.

It's important to note that during the same month that Mac and I were digging into the facts of that radio interview, Al Burris did contact Mac several times. He admitted to knowing Richardson, and he said that Richardson had contacted him with an offer to pull together $50,000. The money was to be used as a direct campaign contribution to Buddy Darden's run for representative of the 8th Congressional District in Georgia. Darden was opposing Kathy McDonald, wife of the late Larry McDonald, who had been killed during a Korean Airlines flight that had strayed into Soviet airspace. Kathy was heavily favored to win the seat. Richardson, according to Burris, had made it clear that the $50,000 would be coming from Larry Flynt. Burris made it clear to us that he flatly refused the $50,000, especially coming from the likes of Larry Flynt, and that Darden's campaign didn't need that kind of help, anyway. Dubbed "the P. T. Barnum of Smut" by some in the media, Flynt had certainly earned himself that distinction. He was quite the ringmaster.

On October 25, Mac got the opportunity to interview Richardson in person, as Cobb County had him in custody and was preparing to ship him down to Orange County, Florida, to answer for probation violation. In that interview, Richardson denied any association with Flynt, any knowledge of a man named Clark Williams, and any involvement whatsoever with any shooting. Later in that same interview, however, he changed his tune with respect to knowing Flynt. He admitted having the $50,000, and he also told us how the money was to be used to work against Kathy McDonald's campaign: a portion of the money was allegedly to go to Ronald Still, the Sheriff of Dade County (in McDonald's district) for publicly coming out in opposition to her election. Richardson added that Flynt had asked him to dig up copies of Kathy and Larry McDonalds' marriage license, as well as to plant cocaine in the car of one of her campaign workers. These were of course allegations that came from a con man, so who knew what was true and what was not? Still, it's interesting to understand the convoluted environment in which we were expected to sift fact from fiction. It was not an easy one in which to find the truth.

I had often wondered whether Larry Flynt really believed the outlandish theories he produced with respect to his shooting. I knew that the damage done by the rifle had left him paralyzed and in excruciating pain for years, and I suppose I deduced from that that he was likely taking some very powerful drugs to alleviate that pain. Perhaps the drugs were clouding his judgment and his reasoning abilities.

I also knew that Larry Flynt loved to aggressively seek out the skeletons discreetly ensconced in the closets of politicians and right-wing conservatives throughout the country. His reasoning for doing this digging, he said, was to expose hypocrisy, which he was fond of saying was the "enemy of democracy." Personally, I believe he was solely interested in boosting sales of his magazine, but that is just my opinion.

I know firsthand the time and effort that went into investigating the case of the shooting of Flynt and Reeves, hence my assertion that Flynt had no grounds on which to base his accusations and wild suppositions. Normally I wouldn't give a second thought to the rantings of a man like Larry Flynt. But I am passionate about the truth, and about finding it.

From what I understand, Flynt is still mentally sharp these days, and he continues to run his massive corporation from the vantage point of a Beverly Hills office.

CHAPTER 21
Our Sins Come Home to Roost

"FIFTEEN, TWENTY, TWENTY-FIVE," Hell yeah. *I'll be eating good tonight.*
Joe Franklin continued counting out his hard-earned cash, for which
he had just exchanged a pint of his blood. His luck was finally turning, after that near miss in Kentucky. He could feel it. Still, something didn't feel right. He couldn't put his finger on it, but he had
learned a long time ago to trust his gut, and his gut was uneasy. The
warm Florida sun shone down on him, and a faint October breeze
ruffled the bills he held in his hand. What could possibly be wrong?

"Get on your knees. Now!" Franklin stopped short; a couple of
five-dollar bills fell from his hand, fluttering away down the sidewalk as the wind pushed them along. For a moment, he was sure
the man was talking to someone else. And in the next moment, he
understood the uneasiness he had been feeling. Once again, his gut
had been right.

"Place your hands on top of your head!" No, they were talking to
him, all right. There were six guns pointed at him, and behind every
one of them was a man who looked as though he'd have no problem
opening fire. Assessing the situation in just a matter of seconds, he
decided that running would be suicide. Instead, he interlaced his
fingers and placed his hands atop his head, sinking to his knees

onto the warm concrete. He watched two more of his hard-earned five-dollar bills flutter free, tumbling and skipping away in the sunshine and teasing breeze of a fall day in Florida. He decided it best not to go running after them.

An FBI agent, the one who had barked the instructions for him to get on his knees, approached him with a half-run, half crab-walk, sideways and with his gun still trained on Franklin's chest. The other agents stood back with their weapons raised, daring him to twitch or even to sneeze. When the crab-walking agent reached him, he pulled out his handcuffs with one hand, opened them, and slipped one cuff around Franklin's thin wrist. The customary crowd was gathering and for once, they didn't seem to mind approaching the scene. Curiosity is a funny thing with people. They just can't help themselves, and it always seemed like the more dangerous the spectacle, the more curious they got.

He could hear sirens in the distance, but he didn't know whether they were intended for him or for some other lucky fellow.

Joseph Paul Franklin, the murderer and bank robber, had been caught and when push came to shove, that fact boiled down to just two things. When the FBI began noticing similarities in otherwise random and unrelated cases, Joseph Franklin's name, or one of his numerous aliases, kept turning up. Of all the information shared and divulged at that law enforcement conference in Cincinnati, Franklin's tattoos, and his habit of selling his blood for money in between bank robberies, are what finally got him caught. It was as simple, and as insignificant, as that.

Utah had the first shot at him, for murdering those two young men at Liberty Park. For the next two decades, though, Joseph Franklin faced legal action across the US, eventually being convicted of eight murders, and tried and acquitted for shooting Vernon Jordan. He loved telling that tale too, because on several occasions, he openly and proudly admitted to shooting the civil rights leader.

Despite all the convictions in various states, Joe remained in the federal penitentiary in Marion, Illinois, because of the tight security measures. He was sentenced to life in prison in several states, but then it was Missouri's turn. The prosecutors over there had no intention of looking the other way on the Gerald Gordon shooting. Missouri wanted blood, an eye for an eye. Joseph Franklin was tried and convicted of the Gerald Gordon shooting in the synagogue parking lot, and the result of that conviction was not just another life sentence tacked onto the six or seven that he already faced. Missouri is a death penalty state.

Other states continued to pursue convictions for murders, and once those trials were complete, Franklin would have theoretically been indicted for bombings and bank robberies, too. After a while, though, there seemed to be no point in adding years to a man's penance that he could not possibly serve. Even in Georgia, where he had finally been indicted for shooting Larry Flynt and Gene Reeves, the District Attorney declined to prosecute the case. "We knew that he'd never get out of prison, and when Missouri got him, we knew he'd be put to death. We had no intention of bringing the circus to town by trying Franklin for (the shootings), spending a lot of taxpayer money, and risking an escape attempt," said Danny Porter, Gwinnett County's District Attorney, in 2013.

Joe Franklin would live out the last fifteen years of his life in the dismal prison in Bonne Terre, Missouri. The transfer from Marion to Bonne Terre did not afford him the chance to escape; rather, the calculated risk that he took in confessing to a murder committed in a death penalty state got him just that—the death penalty, and no more. "Our sins always come home to roost," he could hear his mother's raspy voice croaking, even now as he sat on death row. He wished she'd stop popping into his head. He hated her as much today as he did when he was that small, scared boy hiding under the porch. Maybe more.

In the end, the Missouri conviction was the only one that mattered to Joe with respect to consequences. Oh sure, he'd love to have gotten just half a chance to escape from prison while he served all those life sentences (or as many as he possibly could before he died of old age). But to know that you're going to die, and where, and why, and how, well now that was a horse of a different color. It gave a man pause to think. Toward the end of his life, when interview requests from reporters became more frequent, Franklin was sure to tell them that he was not treated fairly when he stood trial for killing Gerald Gordon. "I wasn't in my right mind. I was mentally ill. The abuse and malnutrition at the hands of my mother messed me up. I didn't get to tell anybody that." This claim became his mantra, and his attorneys said that they were trying to appeal his sentence based on that oversight, but they got nowhere with the effort.

Sitting on death row, Joe Franklin got religion, as the folks down South are fond of saying. He said that he had studied the Bible while in prison, had memorized scriptures, and that reading (combined with some intense therapy) had shown him the error of his ways. It seemed that, when it came to his own precious life, he wasn't any too thrilled to be giving it up in exchange for some long-ago crimes for which he'd repented and said he was sorry. He had gotten right with Jesus, and Jesus taught forgiveness, not condemnation. These days, Joe leaned more toward Jesus Christ's way of looking at things, and farther away from the mean and vengeful God of the Old Testament. These days, the Jewish God struck fear in whatever heart Joe Franklin had left. With that angle in mind, that of forgiveness and even-handed justice, he stated clearly in several pre-execution interviews that he would still kill a man who harmed a child without giving it a second thought, and he wished he would have killed both Eric Harris and Dylan Klebold before they ever got the chance to shoot up Columbine high school and its students. To Joe, that seemed like a Jesus-like thing to say.

Joe Franklin had a date with the state of Missouri—November 20, 2013, to be exact. There was something very sobering about knowing that he would die on that date, at the hands of someone that would clock in to work that day, just there to do his job. He had fifteen years to think about that, too. *I hope that fucker gets paid more than minimum wage. I'd hate for him to screw it up.*

Fifteen years looks pretty short when it's in the rearview mirror, and before he knew it, November 2013 had arrived. His days were, quite literally, numbered. And because of that, another phenomenon was taking place as the date of his death approached. Joseph Franklin was becoming somewhat of a celebrity. Everyone, from CNN to the small newspapers in the towns where he had murdered innocent citizens, wanted to talk to him. It seemed that Joe Franklin had finally gained some notoriety for himself, and in circumstances that might have driven another man to his knees in sorrow and repentance, he was enjoying the limelight immensely.

CHAPTER 22
Put to Rest
(2013)

AT 6:07. A.M., the worn and wrinkled man swallowed hard and closed his eyes, waiting for sweet sleep to overtake him. There were others in the room with him, watching and waiting, but he stared straight ahead, unblinking, at the cracked and stained ceiling. His thoughts took a hard left, toward unexpected images of his childhood home; blinking hard against those jagged memories, he opened his eyes again and studied the ceiling of the killing room. Not much had changed up there in the last minute or so.

Strangely, Joseph Paul Franklin felt nothing, except perhaps a small measure of relief now that the end was truly in sight. No guilt. No regrets, despite the tear-jerking stories of salvation and solemn vows of having turned from his wicked ways. He had happily shared these accounts with the media vultures over the past few weeks, hungrily lapping up the attention and publicity that they bought him. The ravenous reporters had flocked to him like geese swarming a child with a handful of bread crusts. They couldn't get enough of whatever he scattered.

Is Lori out there? he wondered. He had thought more about his daughter in the past couple of months than he could ever recall, perhaps because the final season of his life was bearing down on him. In truth, Franklin wasn't really that old; he was only sixty-three, in fact. Practically a spring chicken, as his mother used to say, *may her soul still be blazing in hell.* But years of living hard, nursing hatred, and running from the law had slowly but surely taken their toll on him. Lines and crevices were etched deep into his tired face, and his scraggly hair (which had grown wild and well past his collar near the end, but what difference did that make?) was mottled with shades of gray and white. Today, he wore it tucked behind his ears. He had also chosen to wear his black-rimmed glasses to the death chamber; they had slipped slightly askew while the guards were strapping his limbs to the gurney and the doctor prepared him for this, his final act, a real showstopper. The spectacles almost made him look scholarly, like a college professor perhaps, but a closer look at the hard miles on his face told another story.

Under the thin white sheet, the man strained against the wide restraining straps, a subconscious effort to contradict the reality that was bearing down on him, soon to devour him whole. He tightened one arm and made a fist, the blurred image of the blue-green grim reaper tattoo shifting slightly over the taut muscles. Faded blue-green drops of blood dripped from the reaper's scythe; as he relaxed his arm, so the reaper relaxed. There was no point in fighting his confinement or the situation itself. His fate had been sealed, just as he had sealed the fates of so many during his three-year killing mission. The outcome today was inevitable, and while his mind was still quite disciplined, ancient instincts still whispered in his ear to flee, to run away before it was too late.

The straps that bound his arms were his reality now; the blurry grim reaper was a mere shadow of a past and very faint passion that had once burned white-hot, one man's battle cry for an all-out race war. Some, including a retired lawman down in Georgia, believe that the passion burned as hot on the day of his execution as it did three decades ago.

Joe had told one reporter just the day before that the foreboding image on his arm signified the fact that he was at war, and that the

survival of the white race was at stake. No, this was no college professor lying prone under the sickly-green lighting of a bank of fluorescent tubes here in the killing room; the circumstances in which
Joseph Franklin found himself this November morning would belie
the unlikely comparison between himself and a mild-mannered
scholar. While this man could have, perhaps in another life, taken
the path to become an educator—a reaper and sharer of knowledge—in this life, he had chosen to shoulder the roles of judge, jury,
and executioner.

No one except he knew exactly how many times he had killed in
ice cold blood (he had recently admitted to "approximately twenty-
two," but he couldn't be sure), and several other states had convicted
him of the crime of murder, but Missouri was the first state that
wanted to kill him for it, sort of their way of returning the favor. He
had been sitting on death row for fifteen years now, removed from
society by incarceration for more than thirty years, over half his
life. In all that time, he supposed he had never really believed that
this day would come. He had worked the system and played the
bleeding heart attorneys and activists like tightly strung fiddles for
so long, he never truly thought it would end—not like this, anyway.
He had never given much thought to what he might say or eat or
even think on his last day among the living, seeing as how he never
thought that he'd be parting company with them to answer for his
many crimes. Even as he waited in a small, windowless cell for his
attorney's appeals to either gain traction or be shot down by some
sleep-deprived judge somewhere in Missouri, he never gave those
petty considerations much room in his head. He hadn't had time to
think about what thoughts to pack up and take with him as he lay
on what was now, without question, his deathbed. As a result, he
uttered no last statement and ate no last meal in that final lonely
cell on the final leg of his last walk in Bonne Terre, Missouri. He
just sat there with his attorney, the warden, and the chaplain, seemingly still believing on some level that the wheels that had been set
in motion would somehow grind to a lumbering halt, that he would

be escorted back to his own cell on the main block, and that he would be allowed to play puppeteer with the media and with law enforcement agencies as he had become accustomed during these many years.

The phone call would come, and it would be the judge on the line, the judge unlucky enough to be standing watch that night, the judge who didn't want blood on his hands. He would utter the words that would put an end to all this. Everyone would breathe a collective sigh of relief, and life as Joseph Paul Franklin had known it for so long would go on.

And yet here he lay, and the black phone over there that looked so out of place still sat silent. It had not been placed there for making outgoing calls. It had no rotary dial, no buttons on its face. No, that phone was there only to receive a call, one that every death row inmate hoped would come when it was his turn to bid the world farewell. If that phone rang, it would be the governor. It would mean that the execution had been halted, for now anyway. Today, however, the phone sat there silent, mocking him. Without warning, a line from an old Randy Travis song popped into his head, the irony so sharp that it made his head hurt. Something about the phone still not ringing, so it still must not be her, or something along them lines. One of them lines that was so dumb it was smart. Had it not been for the direness of his situation, Franklin would have busted out laughing at that one. Under the circumstances, though, he just allowed a slight smile to curl his thin lips. He'd trade places with ol' Randy right about now, that much was for sure. Aside from the random song lyrics that had flitted in, then out without warning, he could muster no other thoughts to take his mind off that malevolent needle and thin, clear tube that snaked under the sheet and into his arm, put there for the singular purpose of doing some very black business. No thoughts to take his mind off of that one-way mirror and the people sitting just the other side of it.

He could have spoken, could have said his "I'm sorrys" and "Please forgive mes" to the people sitting in the gallery who were there to perform their gruesome, voyeuristic duty to the state, but he just didn't seem to have it in him. *To hell with all of them. I ain't sorry.*

In fact, he had shared with another reporter just a day or two ago that the only thing he was truly sorry about was that it wasn't legal to kill niggers and Jews. That statement conflicted with another he had given to a different news reporter on the same day, one that begged the forgiveness of his victims' families. *So stupid, and so easily manipulated. I think I'll miss that the most, holding court with those idiots in the press.* He spoke, and they came running. Hell, he practically had his own phone line and his own office in the prison, especially there toward the end. He had talked to reporters more than he had his own family, once the date for his execution had been set. Of course, that wasn't saying much.

Not even twenty-four hours ago, one of the guards had asked him for his autograph on a crumpled dinner napkin. Obligingly, he scrawled his name right next to a spot of smeared spaghetti sauce. Around here, he was a fucking celebrity all right. *You'd best believe that.*

And from out of the blue, Franklin felt a singular stabbing pang of loneliness, wanting only the familiar comfort of the dark, cool hiding place that was his as a child. He would crawl under there to escape the unhappy reality of his childhood. He would escape his mother's wrath under there, he would eat his stolen food under there without fear of discovery, and he would step willingly into the fantasy world that his beloved books opened up for him. *Old habits really do die hard.* At that last thought, one single tear welled, then streamed slowly from his left eye and dissolved into his graying hairline. Was he feeling sorrow? No, likely not. He was feeling the impact of the end of a life lived for hatred and a soul spurred on for one single purpose: killing, to pit white men against black men, to eradicate an entire race. He was feeling the full weight of a life empty, wasted.

Had he been sitting up, Franklin's shoulders would have been curved and hunched from the weight of carrying around an almost unbearable burden from the very first day he was pushed forth screaming and crying into this vile world. Hate weighs an awful lot, and it gets bigger and heavier with age.

Had his hands been free as he lay there on the metal table, he would have subconsciously tucked his hair behind his left ear and adjusted his glasses, a habit he had developed nearly fifty years ago as a nervous young man who was already being schooled in loneliness, hate, and retribution. Then he would have wiped the tear in anger, because weakness repulsed him.

Franklin took another deep breath, then closed his eyes, trying to conjure up an image that he might take with him into the hereafter. Surely a man deserved at least one pleasant thought, all his own, as he exited this earth. He tried to envision a picture of one of his long-ago wives; he attempted to summon thoughts of his daughter, but nothing would materialize out of his dark mind to bring him comfort, not even for a moment. He settled on summoning some of his favorite passages from *Mein Kampf*, Hitler's manifesto, the only real Bible Franklin had ever lived by as a young man. *Mein Kampf*. "My Struggle." It was the book that changed his life, set his feet on the path that led to this room on death row in a Missouri prison. It was too hard to focus, and he couldn't remember even the simplest, most profound passages. He searched his mind and his heart for anything, anything at all, but all that seemed to appear were the bad things, the things that had gotten him here in the first place. The things that Missouri Governor Jay Nixon had called "merciless acts of violence, fueled by hate," right before he denied the defense's request for clemency. *Well at least there's that. When I'm gone, so are the bad things.* Having been behind bars for more than three decades and trapped inside a head riddled with hatred and persecution for as long as he could remember, good memories were few and far between. He'd just have to make do.

Now, he regretted refusing his last meal. He thought he had been driving home a point by doing that, but lying here, with no pleasant thoughts to console him as his life faded unwillingly to a tiny white dot, soon to be swallowed by black nothingness, he wished he hadn't turned it down. Even right here and now, trussed up like a bespectacled Thanksgiving turkey, he believed he could eat a whole fried chicken, gobs of mashed potatoes swimming in milk gravy, a whole pan of cornbread (no sense in worrying about eating green vegetables for heart health at that meal, was there?), and a big slab of cherry pie with soft vanilla ice cream. Not only could he have eaten that and more a couple of hours ago, he could have been thinking about that glorious meal now. As it was, he didn't even have the memory of a good meal to escort him into heaven. Or hell. *I guess I'll know the answer to that one soon enough.* He felt however, in the pit of his stomach, that he knew exactly what the answer was. Images of flames and a red-hot pitchfork, the sounds of screams and moans of regret, danced across his consciousness. Memories, no doubt, from all those fire-and-brimstone sermons he heard as a young man, as he trolled various religions looking for a home, a family. He pushed the terrifying thoughts down and smothered them, before they took up residence and drove him mad.

How long will this take? Who is out there? he thought again, but he couldn't bring himself to consider much beyond that, and he refused to turn his head toward the large window on the wall beside him. He would not give them the satisfaction.

Out of nowhere (and to his cruel amusement), the film recollecting his life really did begin to play out before him, a jittery, poorly-made, cut-rate film peppered with faces and images he didn't want to see. *So it's true, what they say. Your life does rewind right in front of you, just before you die.* Conversations among doomed men tend to stray into the realm of the bizarre and, inevitably, the morose. His colleagues on death row could start a conversation on just about any topic that came to mind, but that conversation would inevitably end on a morbid note. Death was on everyone's mind, all the time:

"Wonder what it feels like to die?"

"Wonder what goes through your mind at the end?" Things like that.

Well there's another good thing. This would be the last time he'd have to think those thoughts, push down the parade of faces of the people whose lives he had extinguished like so many half-smoked cigarettes.

Fruitless appeals and two brief stays of execution had brought a glimmer of hope and a few added hours to this otherwise dismal situation in his last couple of days, but the appeals had fallen apart almost as quickly as they had materialized. As a result, so had the fragile stays of execution. Those human rights idiots and the whiny death penalty opponents had jumped all over the fact that the use of pentobarbital alone (a drug similar to propofol, made famous a few years ago by the late, great Michael Jackson), purchased from a secret compounding pharmacy located somewhere in the great US of A, might cause him undue pain and suffering. The drug might be contaminated, the protestors said. The more humane protocol, according to the liberal attorneys and the crybaby human rights activists, was a lethal combination of three drugs, but the European Union had objected to the use of the three medications for executions in the US, threatening to limit sales of the drug as long as capital punishment is allowed in even one state. The medical community got itself in an uproar over the prospect of having limited access to those medicines, because the drugs in question apparently have real and good uses outside of a state prison. Therefore, a procedural change was made in a few states and just like that, Missouri jumped on the bandwagon of using just one drug, straight, for legal executions. Just the month before, in October of 2013, the state's powers-that-be had approved the use of five grams of pentobarbital alone to carry out the death penalty. And for the first time in nearly three years, the state was going to kill a man. Some attorney along the way sat him down and carefully explained all this to him in a manner that one might use when trying to explain atomic fusion to a five-year-old child. He vividly remembered having the urge to lunge across the metal table and choke the life out of that high and mighty bitch as she spoke to him like that, but of course he didn't. No sense buying himself any more trouble, the way he saw it. People were already standing in line to have a shot at pinning more murders on him. He sure wasn't going to make it easy for them.

The long and the short of it was that, despite all the legal wrangling and sleight of hand, today the man would not enjoy the added benefits of having pancuronium bromide (a paralytic agent) and potassium chloride (which stops the heart and causes death) on his side. He'd simply have a whopper of a dose of pentobarbital, an anesthetic used mainly on animals, rarely humans. When the do-gooders looking to make names for themselves had cried "foul," claiming that he would likely experience cruel and unusual suffering as a result of being short-changed the two other drugs, he couldn't help laughing. He privately thought that was the most ridiculous thing he had ever heard (*I ain't going to feel any better about being killed by three drugs instead of one*), but who was he to argue? He was getting the best legal defense the good taxpayers of Missouri could provide, and he was going to go right along with whatever tricks his lawyer might pull out of her overpriced hat at the eleventh hour. In his opinion, the indignantly conscientious objection to the use of one drug was a load of crap, but at that stage of the game, even a few hours of time (six to be exact, as it turned out) was a most precious commodity, and he'd take them. *Bottom line is, dead is dead. I ought to know. I seen enough of it.*

Another appeal had been filed, one that claimed that Franklin was not mentally competent, therefore not able to understand what was about to happen to him. Now that one had really made him chuckle. As far as he was concerned, he was smarter than the whole damned bunch. How else could he have gotten away with everything he did for all that time? *Hell, I had to own up to most of it, or they never would have caught me.* Yes, that argument had made him laugh when he first heard it. Of course, he wasn't laughing now. Nobody was, at least nobody that was here for the grave final chapter in what had turned out to be a puzzling and rather frightening book.

Where the rubber met the road, the higher-ups in Missouri didn't give a rat's ass about killing people in a responsibly humane or cowardly anonymous manner. In a nutshell, the state maintained that if it was the people's job to kill a man, then it was their business as to how they did it. The simplest, cheapest way to get there was all that interested them. Even in death, it seemed, the now infamous man would again make the six o'clock news and blaze a trail for the other misguided souls that would follow him to this stark killing room in years to come. Seems those dramatic last-minute snatches from the bony fingers of death only happen on TV and in the movies.

A strong but slight man, Franklin looked thin and even frail strapped to a prison gurney with a white sheet pulled up to his chin. He tried again to muster an image to escort him into the gaping maw of the afterlife. *Should I say a prayer? Would it make any difference? And who the hell should I pray to?* As he had heard so many times in prison from fellow inmates (most of them stupid and brutish, but beggars couldn't be choosers), the "electric chair" has brought more men to God than any fire-and-brimstone preacher could hope to save in a lifetime. Now, somehow, the joke didn't seem to be so funny. In fact, it seemed to be true. *All this for killing a Jew. Ain't this life a bitch?*

Without giving the viewing audience (six people the government had picked out—*how's that for a bad ending?)* the satisfaction of moving a muscle or batting an eye, the man tried, weakly at first, to pray to a God that he had never really known. Oh, he was well acquainted with an angry, wrathful, vengeful God, one that was just waiting for His subjects to misstep by way of sinning. But the prison preacher (who came to see him last night and spent the wee hours of this morning with him) had talked to him about a different kind of God, one who loved His children and who was kind. Of course that was just the bullshit they said to try to make you feel better right before they shot you up with bargain-basement poison, but what else could he hold onto now, stretched out and strapped down under a glaring fluorescent light, like a twisted sideshow attraction at a traveling carnival? *Ain't this life a bitch.* Out of the corner of his eye, he thought he saw the shadow of the black curtains on the other side of that one-way mirror swing closed. He supposed he knew what that meant but again, strangely, he couldn't bring himself to care. Tired. So tired.

His mind was muddled now, fuzzy. His heartbeat slowed, thudding and thumping irregularly, like a rusty old clunker that had thrown a rod. A prayer would not come, but he no longer thought it was that important; he just wanted to go to sleep. He wanted to rest. Instinctively, he fought hard to clear his mind. Had to stay sharp. Had to be smarter than them even now. They had told him before they did it, before the executioner had pushed the poison into his thin arm. They had told him that the execution was going forward, and they were going to "administer the drug." He wished they hadn't told him that. It was probably a legal thing, so his family couldn't sue the state or something. There was always a logical reason and a legal justification for everything they did to you in prison, even when they were killing you.

He could feel his heart slowing, feel it weakening and sputtering. His pulse was thready and timid, then fast and hard. His heart slammed in his chest as if pounding to get out, as if it sensed a very real danger from something that was in there with it. Or maybe that was the executioner's finger tapping on the gurney next to his head, as he waited impatiently for the pentobarbital to do its dark work. *Jew bastard probably has a tee time this morning.* It was hard to tell where the noise came from, hard to focus. *That damned thumping.*

Reluctantly embracing the sedative's certain effects, Joseph Paul Franklin breathed deep, two more times, then breathed no more. His thoughts unlaced themselves and floated free, slowly falling away until there simply were no more. His chest rose and fell, rose again, then sank deep with an exhale that gave the impression that there was less of him under the bleached sheet than there was just a minute ago. The sinister potion had raced through his veins and done its job cleanly and efficiently, just as the state of Missouri had claimed right up to the end that it would do. If any last thoughts occurred to him as he took his last breath, the somber onlookers couldn't tell. The haggard-looking sixty-three year old looked as though he had simply nodded off to sleep after a big Sunday supper, save for the wide red straps that bound him to the table, and of course, the tubes and wires that snaked under the sheet and ended up both in and on his body. Just like that, Joseph Franklin became the thirty-fifth murderer put to death in the United States in 2013.

There had been no convulsing, no thrashing around, nothing like he had seen before and even enjoyed so many times in his favorite movies. He had simply slipped away, whatever was left of his soul departing unceremoniously for parts unknown.

The prison's attending physician approached his motionless body, listening for a heartbeat and feeling for a pulse; finding neither, he officially pronounced the man dead, an unremarkable end to a rather remarkable life, depending on whom you asked. It was exactly 6:17 a.m.

Watching a person die plays all kinds of tricks on the mind. The deceased can appear to continue to breathe, or perhaps furrow a brow or twitch an ankle or wrist. Of course, the dead know they're dead. It's just those who are left behind who seem to have trouble registering that fact. Nevertheless, one of the country's most notorious serial killers took his last breath, then gave it back, in the very early morning of November 20, 2013. Three members of the press and three private citizens stood witness to the last killing in a line of many in which Joseph Paul Franklin had headlined. At long last, he had paid the price for his sins, however many there were, that Missouri had demanded he pay. The murderer who had escaped capture for so many years slipped quietly out of this world and into the next. Many, including Det. Cowart, believe to this day that Joe Franklin went to his grave knowing exactly the number of lives he snuffed out, and knowing the exact nature of the crimes with which he was never charged but did indeed commit. With him, he took some very dark secrets, indeed.

CHAPTER 23
Back to the Basement
(2014)

Detective Michael Cowart

In this, the retelling of the investigation of Joseph Paul Franklin and more specifically, the shooting of Larry Flynt and Gene Reeves, I have dredged up memories that I believed had been cold and gray, buried forever. I did it reluctantly at first, but then the telling became somewhat cathartic, and I allowed the memories to flow. The human mind is an amazing thing, terribly sharp and efficient when it has to be, and comfortingly soft and foggy when it wants to be. I suppose I should be glad that the memories did come back to me as readily as they did, once they started coming. Many men my age cannot say the same.

I have recounted all the stories about Joseph Paul Franklin that I care to, all that I have in me to tell. Are there a few more rattling around in that box somewhere? Maybe. But they are not necessary to this accounting, so I will leave them where they lie, sleeping.

I read an article, or perhaps I had seen a news story, about the man's pending execution in November 2013. He is dead and gone now. As with every twisted offender with whom I have come in contact over the years, I could not help back then and even now, wondering what Joe Franklin might have become given different circumstances. He was a very bright man, without a doubt. He was obviously focused and dedicated. What might he have become had he been born to loving parents, had he not been poor, had he not been injured and outcast? Ah well, these musings are just that. Musings. Pointless meaderings of a man who thinks too much, I'm afraid.

At the end, many (including himself, depending on the day and the interviewer) believed that he had sincerely renounced his evil ways and his resolute hatred of blacks, Jews, and the mixing of races. How do I know that? In his last few days on earth as a living, breathing man, he must have had his own little office inside the Missouri prison, complete with a desk and telephone. Reporters clamored for some time with him, and he loved the heat of the spotlight. He bathed in it right up until the very end. He would swear to one reporter that he had come to know Jesus Christ and had repented of his wicked sins. He would tell another that he had no regrets, save one. He wished that it had been legal to kill "niggers and Jews," and that he was still able to do it. For what it's worth, I would like to share just one more observation about Joe that I will take to my grave believing wholeheartedly.

No matter what he told reporters as he held court from death row in Missouri, Joe never changed. He never softened. He never truly renounced his wicked deeds or his hatred for other races. When he was executed, he had spent more years in prison than he had spent as a free man. He was incarcerated at age thirty, and thirty-three years later, he was executed. He spent every single one of those thirty-three years in solitary confinement, partly because he was so hated by other inmates, and partly because he was such a high escape risk. Some say that he truly did repent and change his ways, that all the hatred had drained right out of him while he sat in prison, reading books and talking to therapists about his feelings. Having spent the entire time in Missouri without ever seeing a television, he became a voracious reader. He liked to tell reporters that he was a better-read man than most college professors, and maybe that was true. I do know that Joe was not a stupid man; rather, he was far from it. Did all that reading enlighten him? Some say it did. Still others said that spending over half of his life in solitary confinement had driven him mad. They said that he had softened because he had lost the mental edge that he had sharpened on the hard whetstone of hatred.

I know better, and I'll tell you why. I looked straight into Joe Franklin's eyes on more than one occasion. I watched an interview or two that had been conducted near the end of his life, and of one thing I am absolutely certain. Joe was not a changed man. He had not gone soft in the head. Right up to the end, he seemed to have one thing on his mind, besides saving his own neck, that is. That one thing was his mission.

It appeared he was waiting, waiting for someone to blink, to fall asleep at the switch. A guard perhaps, or one of the officers who escorted him from one hearing to the next. I believed that he was waiting, biding his time, but always watching. And if that guard had blinked, or if the officer had turned his back for even a minute, Joe Franklin would have been gone. He would have slipped away into the chilly darkness of a Utah night, or simply vanished in the sweltering heat of a Tennessee summer day. Joseph Franklin was a ghost, and a malevolent one at that. He was consumed with hatred, motivated by a need for revenge that even he did not understand completely. The phenomenon that was Joseph Paul Franklin, or James Clayton Vaughn, or James A. Cooper, or any one of the dozens of identities he flashed as he slithered through life, was the result of a perfect storm of terrible circumstances and events. When he was executed on November 20, 2013, he settled all accounts as best he could, with whatever currency he had left. One piece of paper was mailed to the district attorney's office in Gwinnett County just a few days later. That piece of paper officially closed the case that had been open in Gwinnett since March 6, 1978. It read, simply, that the named defendant, Joseph Paul Franklin, had been executed on November 20, 2013. Several other jurisdictions received that same document, and several other boxes of files were closed, loaded onto a hand truck, and trundled off to basements in their respective courthouses. The rest, perhaps, Franklin's God will see to. I suppose we'll never know.

To the best of my knowledge, Joe's place of burial is unknown. It's probably best that way, all things considered. To some, Joe's grave would serve as a monument to bravery, patriotism, and white supremacy; to others, it would represent the shame and sorrow in which the long list of the South's transgressions is steeped. When he was buried, he took with him his hatred, and he left a wide wake of sorrow and destruction behind him. By his hand, families were destroyed, young lives were cut short, and communities had been shaken. His life and his deeds were very much like the violent springtime storms, so common in his birthplace of Alabama, that give birth to wild, whipping tornadoes. Twisters are powerful and unpredictable; the randomness with which one touches down and wipes out an entire town, and another spins itself harmlessly back up into the heavens, is terrifying. Joe Franklin's life was a tragic perfect storm of circumstances, one that began in Alabama and cut a swath of devastation through several states, and through many lives.

As I was packing away my files, having perused every transcript and police report in them, I realized that I nearly forgot to mention one last twist to this story, already so full of turns and surprises. I found it interesting, as Joe's date of execution approached, that Larry Flynt himself came out of the woodwork to urge clemency for the man who shot him. Although Franklin ended Flynt's life as he knew it on March 6, 1978, Flynt publicly made it clear that he did not want his shooter to be put to death. A surprising opinion, I thought, but then again, I suppose nothing really surprises me anymore. I recall that Flynt, always the ultra-liberal, anti-authority figure, said that he doesn't support capital punishment because it has not been proven to deter crime. Capital punishment, according to Flynt, fulfills one purpose only, and that is man's need for revenge. It teaches no lessons, sets no moral precedents. I do remember reading somewhere that Flynt said he wouldn't mind having an hour alone in a room with Joe and a pair of wire cutters and pliers, so that he could inflict the same damage on his shooter as he had endured. Reading that, I almost felt sorry for Flynt. All the money in the world, posh Beverly Hills offices, private airplanes, women, and even a gold-plated wheelchair, I figured, could never replace the use of his legs. I almost felt sorry for him.

EPILOGUE

SIXTY-THREE YEARS BEFORE his death, James Clayton Vaughn was born to parents who were sick, cruel, and abusive without mercy. He was born into abject poverty, in a time and a place in the southern United States that was roiling with upheaval, resentment, and open hatred between blacks and whites. Once a little boy who dreamed of someday becoming a police officer, Jimmy Vaughn, a.k.a. Joseph Franklin, instead grew to be a despicable monster, prowling and stalking most of his victims purely at random. Was he a hopeless victim and product of his circumstances, or was he an evil man bent on killing and with a clear vision of his precious race war? There are arguments on both sides, and they continue even today.

Now having completed the writing of the text, I have the unique ability to reflect on the process of learning the details of Joseph Paul Franklin's life and death. A man only has one life to give to the state in exchange for his crimes, but Franklin was responsible for many more shootings, killings, and robberies than that one in the parking lot of a Jewish temple. He was a ruined man. In retrospect, several experts opined that he did not so much choose the path that he walked; rather, he simply pursued a destiny that had been predetermined by the circumstances of his life and the volatility of his environment. I took liberties as I wrote about his last thoughts; of course, no one knew exactly what they were, as he refused to even make a final statement just before keeping his appointment with the Reaper. However, through months of research and extensive interviews with people who knew him firsthand, I drew what are admittedly my own conclusions about his final thoughts. My assumptions, though, are based on this research and these interviews. In doing this, I attempted to convey my perception of the man's humanity as he faced the hereafter. No matter how many atrocities a man commits in his time on this earth, I believe that he was at one time an innocent child. I believe that while we are all ultimately accountable for our sins, some of us were dealt a hand that no one could play for good. I also believe that Joseph Paul Franklin was one of those people.

Something else that I found is that there are curious similarities between Joseph Franklin and his famous March 1978 target, Larry Flynt. They were both born and raised in the South. They were born into painfully poor environments, well below the poverty level. They are (or were, in Franklin's case) intelligent men. And both men sought answers, or perhaps absolution, in religion. Yet their lives were on almost perpendicular trajectories. What was the difference between the two? To be sure, they both battled fierce demons. And while the debate, for most, comes full circle to simply the question of nature versus nurture, some of the old-timers who have gone before would explain both men's torment quite simply. It was "born into" them. They were both Southern men, and the anguish is in the soil.

The division, ignorance, and poverty that seeded the fertile agricultural South in the years following the signing of the Thirteenth Amendment spread far and wide. Even with the abolition of slavery in 1865 and the gruesome, drawn-out tragedy that was the US Civil War, Abraham Lincoln could not unearth what had taken generations to take root in the South.

Dr. Martin Luther King gave his life in the battle to overcome racial mistrust and hatred. His effort was a valiant one, but ultimately, he too failed to overcome hate. Some would dispute that claim, strictly out of reverence and respect for the late Dr. King. Others might look no farther than Dr. King's own children, who bicker and argue over the monument to the man, as well as over his letters and papers. His dream shone brightly during his lifetime, and his wife sustained a valiant effort to carry the torch after his death, but even the dream was drowned out by division, and hate, and the lust for money and power. As long as race is held as a playing card that trumps accountability, responsibility, and intent, there will be racial division, greed, and the violence that accompanies them both.

There are some who say that in another generation or two, there will be no more evidence of racial hatred in America, even in the South. While that notion is an unlikely one (it is difficult to erase resentment and mistrust that are passed on from parent to child), it is a worthy dream. Nothing good can ever come from hate. If Joseph Franklin taught us nothing else, he taught us that.

Today, there is cultural and racial diversity in the South to be sure; even in the Deep South live not only blacks and whites, but also Latinos, Asians, Europeans, Arabs, and others from all over the world. In Gwinnett County, Georgia, alone, there are more than one hundred seventy-seven languages and dialects spoken by its inhabitants. People from all over the world have come here for the inviting climate and the promising economy. These people work and live side by side. They coexist. They build lives and families, businesses and homes.

But they are building all those things on Southern soil. Yes, the days of cotton empires and sprawling plantations are long gone. Technology and industry now thrive where once there were only crops of cotton, and second only to cotton, peanuts. But the soil remains the same. And out of that soil has sprung a generation and an industry with the same roots in ignorance and hatred as the South of 1865, and of the 1950s, '60s, and '70s. This new generation is seeded in the same warm, fertile Southern soil that birthed cotton and her mean sister, slavery. From that soil sprung the Ku Klux Klan, the National States Rights party, and clever, greedy politicians and rabble-rousers who trade in fear and mistrust. Hate groups, or just hate in general, are sold on dark street corners and in the hot, unforgiving sunshine of a mid-summer day in Georgia, or in Alabama. Hate is sown and nurtured in communities, in schools, and in homes, around dinner tables. It is marketed to millions on the evening news. Sadly, this generation is seeded with hate mongers, with those who have made quite a comfortable living pitting blacks against whites, drawing on the power of the resentment and mistrust sown ages ago in that same soil. They are lucrative industries, race baiting and hate brokering—just as lucrative, some might say, as cotton once was.

Joseph Paul Franklin was a conjuring of our darkest fears and ugliest truths. His actions cannot be blamed on drug addiction or alcohol abuse, mental illness or injury. The blame lies squarely on the shoulders of hate and racial division, on his parents, on poverty, and on the man himself. There will always be the possibility of another Joseph Paul Franklin rising from Southern soil, as long as there is profit to be made from the peddling of hate.

In a 2013 interview that Franklin granted eight days before his execution, the convicted murderer shared an insight with a curious reporter who seemed to amuse him, even as he faced the sure date and time of his execution. When the interviewer asked him why he shot Larry Flynt, he answered good-naturedly, "Remember that song by the Charlie Daniels Band? It was called 'The Devil Went Down to Georgia.' I was really into country music back in the seventies, and that song came out about a year after I shot him. I really liked it."

"So, you're saying that you were the devil that went down to Georgia?" the reporter asked.

"Naw, man," he answered, sounding a bit surprised. "Flynt was."

Evil, it seems, is in the eye of the beholder.

"Those who fail to remember the past are doomed to repeat it."
—*George Santayana,*
Spanish philosopher and novelist

THE END

Research Sources

Police reports, interviews, FBI profiles
Source: Gwinnett County District Attorney's office

Lawrenceville (GA) Police Department

The People vs. Larry Flynt, **film,** written by Scott Alexander and Larry Karaszewski, directed by Milos Forman.

Interviews with the late **Gene Reeves** (Flynt's Georgia attorney in the obscenity trial that took place in Gwinnett County), **Det. Michael Cowart** (lead investigator on the case), **Dr. Bagheri** (first surgeon, Button Gwinnett Hospital, credited with saving Flynt's life), and **Paul Cambria,** a member of Flynt's NY legal team that was in Gwinnett County when the shooting happened, and still Flynt's legal counsel. I also talked with townspeople (attorneys, shopkeepers) who were in the area when the shooting happened.

Gwinnett Historical Society archives

People Magazine (vol 14, No. 21), "**On the Trail of a Murderous Sniper Suspect: the Tangled Life of Joseph Paul Franklin,**" by James R. Gaines, Nov. 24, 1980

People Magazine (vol. 7, No. 9), "**There Are People, Says Larry Flynt, Who Want His Mouth Washed Out with Soap,**" by Bill Robinson, March 7, 1977

People Magazine (vol. 9, No. 1,) "**Is Larry Flynt's Conversion for Real—or Just to Escape Prison?**" by Bill Robinson, January 9, 1978

People Magazine (vol. 28, No. 3) "**Her Death Ends the Improbable Love Match of Porn Merchants Althea and Larry Flynt,**" by Michelle Green, July 20, 1987

People Magazine (vol. 20, No. 5) "**Porn Publisher Larry Flynt Beats Drugs but Remains Unashamedly Hooked on Sleaze,**" by Leo Janos, August 1, 1983

Vanity Fair News, '**STRANGE BEDFELLOWS,**' December 19, 2007, 12 am, **The Muckraker's Progress,** by Bruce Handy

The Bryan Times (Bryan, Ohio), March 7, 1978, "**Larry Flynt is in Critical Condition**"